WILLIAMS-SONOMA

MASTERING

Pasta
Noodles & Dumplings

Author
MICHELE SCICOLONE

General Editor
CHUCK WILLIAMS

Photographer
JEFF KAUCK

*f*P
FREE PRESS

NEW YORK · LONDON · TORONTO · SYDNEY

Contents

Mastering Pasta, Noodles & Dumplings offers every reader a cooking class in book form, a one-on-one lesson with a seasoned teacher standing by your side, explaining each recipe step-by-step—with plenty of photographs to illustrate every detail.

Most people think of Italy when they hear the word pasta. There, making pasta is a time-honored family tradition. But since most of us are not blessed with an Italian grandmother to lead us through the intricacies of fettuccine, ravioli, and lasagna, this book is the next best thing. Inside are easy-to-follow lessons that show you how to make, cook, and sauce many classic Italian pasta dishes. Also included are recipes for Asian noodle dishes and dumplings that Western diners have come to enjoy, such as pad thai and pot stickers. Once you've mastered the skills needed to make these recipes, you'll use them all the time.

Here's how this book covers a complete beginning course on pasta, noodles, and dumplings: In the opening pages, you'll find a brief history and an overview of the different types of pasta and of the ingredients you use to make them. This is also where you'll find guidelines on how to cook and serve pasta, noodles, and dumplings. Next, the Basic Recipes chapter includes recipes for three everyday pasta doughs, plus a recipe for an all-purpose white sauce. Then, the Key Techniques chapter provides both photographs and instructions to teach you the essential skills needed to master making pasta, noodles, and dumplings, from rolling out fresh dough and cutting fettuccine to peeling, seeding, and dicing a tomato. Finally, the recipes are divided into three categories—fresh pasta (including ravioli and lasagna), dried pasta, and noodles and dumplings.

The world of pasta is vast. *Mastering Pasta, Noodles & Dumplings* is the road map you need to explore it with confidence.

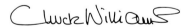

Working with the Recipes

If you're searching for a five-letter word for a food everybody loves, the answer is easy: pasta. It cooks quickly and tastes delicious with even simple sauces, making it a perfect choice for weeknight meals. But this simplicity requires skill. You need to learn how to make pasta, how to cook it well, and how to pair it with first-rate ingredients. Once you've practiced these basics, you'll serve pasta with pride on even the most important occasions.

When learning to make pasta, as with acquiring any new skill, your confidence will increase with practice. This book is designed to take you through that process. Each chapter is anchored with at least one master recipe at the beginning that leads you step-by-step through each stage of cooking. You'll want to make these skill-building recipes first, to ground yourself in the pasta-making tradition.

At first, a recipe may take longer than you imagined, or it may not turn out as you expected. Don't be discouraged;

you'll find the same recipe will come to you more naturally and quickly the next time you make it. Remember, any time you spend in the kitchen is a sound investment in your skills.

Once you've tackled the master recipes, turn to some of the other recipes in the chapters to continue building on your knowledge. Guided by photos illustrating any difficult or confusing aspects, these recipes give you a chance to further expand your skills and recipe repertory, as well as your confidence.

Recipe variations also provide you with a wealth of ways to practice your newly gained skills. For example, once you have mastered Ravioli (page 67) made with a beef filling, you'll have the know-how to make cheese, mushroom, squash, chicken, seafood, and sausage ravioli (pages 72–73), all by changing only a few ingredients. You'll find similar variations throughout this book.

For tips about how to stock your kitchen with basic pasta-making tools and equipment, turn to pages 132–35.

Types of Pasta

Pasta has a distinguished history, comes in many forms, and knows no national boundaries. You'll learn about its variety in the pages ahead: dried spaghetti mixed right in the pan in which you sizzled pancetta for the carbonara sauce (page 102); ribbons of fresh egg pasta tossed in a rich, creamy Alfredo sauce (page 55); and even spicy pad thai with rice noodles and fresh shrimp (page 126). Let these recipes and others take you on an exploration of taste.

A Brief History

Some debate still exists over the true origins of pasta—whether it began in Italy or China. You may recall the popular legend from your grade school days that Marco Polo discovered noodles while traveling in China in the late thirteenth century and brought them back with him to Italy. However, respected historians now agree that Italians and Asians learned how to shape and boil pasta and noodles independently of each other.

Such a conclusion is not surprising, considering the basic recipe for pasta and noodles is one of the simplest you can imagine—often nothing more than flour and water (sometimes with eggs) mixed together to form a dough, and then rolled out and cut into shapes. But, when pasta and noodles are made with care and tossed with a well-matched sauce, the resulting dishes have nearly unrivaled universal appeal.

Today, almost every country in the world incorporates pasta of some type into its cuisine, but the Italians proudly claim pasta as their own. This pride is reflected in pasta's centrality in their diet and in the literally hundreds of specialized—and often fanciful—names they have attached to this favorite food, from *farfalle*, or "butterflies," to *orecchiette*, or "little ears," to *linguine*, or "little tongues."

In the West, we've come to generally associate the word *pasta* with Italian culinary traditions and the word *noodles* primarily with Asian dishes. I've used that distinction in this book, with Pad Thai (page 126) and a recipe for soba (page 117) in the Noodles & Dumplings chapter. You'll find gnocchi and pot stickers there, too.

Italian Traditions

Although many of us consider a heaping dish of Fettuccine Alfredo (page 55) a meal on its own, in Italy pasta typically begins a meal. For example, in Rome, you'll find Spaghetti Carbonara (page 102) listed as a *primo*, or first course, on the menu, rather than as a main dish.

Italians also break down pasta into two categories: *pasta fresca*, "fresh pasta" made from flour and eggs, and *pasta secca*, "dried pasta" made from flour and water. The tradition of fresh pasta comes from northern Italy, where the land is more fertile than in the south, and eggs have been more plentiful and affordable. Here, pasta sauces often call for butter, cream, and rich cheeses, ingredients for which the north is also known.

In southern Italy, dried pasta is more popular, in part for two reasons: eggs were historically less common in the

south, and the cool sea breezes and hot Mediterranean sun are ideal for drying pasta. Olive trees and tomato vines thrive here as well, and you will find a tradition of pasta sauces based on their harvest.

What is important to remember is that Italians don't compare the two or consider one type of pasta to be better than the other. Instead, they understand that fresh and dried pasta are simply different, and directions for cooking and saucing them should respect this difference.

Fresh Pasta

Fresh pasta dough can be made with just a few ingredients: flour, eggs, and sometimes olive oil. When you see Italian grandmothers, or *nonne,* with their slender rolling pins and flour-dusted boards, they are likely preparing to make fresh pasta and then cut it by hand.

Fortunately, you can replicate this labor-intensive method with two modern machines, a food processor and a pasta machine. Most cooks feel these tools do just as good a job as the hand method of the *nonne.*

Fresh pasta is most often cut into the ribbons known as fettuccine, though wider ribbons are also common in Italy such as tagliatelle and *pappardelle.* Fresh egg pasta is also cut into straight or ruffled strips for layering in lasagna, or into small squares for filling and shaping into ravioli and tortellini.

A second type of fresh pasta, made by combining all-purpose (plain) flour and the sturdier semolina flour with salt and water, is popular in southern Italy. You will learn how to make this dough for shaping orecchiette and *cavatelli* (see pages 26, 34, and 35).

Dried Pasta

The fourth chapter in this book is dedicated to dried pastas. The firmness and elasticity of dried pasta come from semolina flour, which is milled from high-protein durum wheat, prized for its particularly hard grains. Dried pastas also owe their golden color to semolina flour.

Extruded in strands or fanciful shapes, dried pastas include spaghetti, linguine, and penne. These staples of the Italian pantry are also regularly found on dining tables outside of Italy, in dishes such as Spaghetti & Meatballs (page 87) and Linguine with Clam Sauce (page 99). Due to its popularity and the fact that it travels so well, high-quality dried pasta is easy to find. For the best results, seek out imported varieties from Italian manufacturers, who cut and shape their pastas with bronze dies (rather than

Other Pasta Traditions

Italians, in addition to pairing dried pasta with olive oil–based sauces and fresh pasta with creamy sauces, adhere to a few other time-honored traditions when serving pasta.

Many Italian restaurants outside Italy offer freshly grated Parmigiano-Reggiano cheese whenever pasta is served. But in Italy, cheese is seldom used with a sauce based on fish or shellfish, and purists also disdain the addition of cheese to a pasta tossed with a game or mushroom sauce.

Red pepper flakes are another ingredient some Italians believe is mismatched with Parmigiano-Reggiano. They would also avoid seasoning a sauce made with red pepper flakes with black pepper, too, since the flavors would compete. Remember: the sauce shouldn't outshine the flavor of the pasta itself. For more information on pairing fresh and dried pastas with sauces, turn to the chart on page 18.

plastic ones). The result is an exceptional pasta with a slightly rough texture perfect for absorbing a sauce.

You can also find fine dried pasta made with eggs. These pastas, often labeled "egg noodles," yield good results, but their flavor is subtler than that of fresh egg pasta. Better manufacturers package their dried egg pasta in nest-shaped coils.

Dumplings

Open almost any international cookbook and you'll find a recipe for dumplings—German spätzle, American chicken and dumplings, Japanese gyoza.

Dumplings take many forms and are close cousins to pasta. Gnocchi, Italy's most celebrated example, are usually made from a potato-based dough that mimics the more traditional wheat pasta dough. Shaped into small "pillows" and boiled, tender gnocchi are often served with the same sauces you use for pasta.

Chinese pot stickers, another type of dumpling, call for wrapping wheat-flour rounds around fillings such as seasoned ground (minced) pork, panfrying them, and then finally steaming them. Instead of saucing pot stickers, you'll want to serve them with a tangy dipping sauce.

Noodles

Noodles are another universal favorite. The term may be used for any kind of long, ribbonlike wheat-flour pasta, especially fresh pasta, but noodles can be made with other types of flour as well. In this book, I've used the term specifically for Asian varieties, though the terms *pasta* and *noodles* can be used interchangeably.

The noodle recipes I've included are adaptations of traditional Asian dishes, although recipes for noodles, especially fresh egg noodles, have a long history in German and Eastern European cooking as well. Inside, you will find Japanese buckwheat soba noodles served cold with a dipping sauce (page 117), delicate Vietnamese rice noodles tossed with a gingery vinaigrette and grilled chicken (page 129), and fresh Chinese wheat noodles served in a spicy peanut sauce (page 130). The wide range of ingredients used to make these recipes will expand your understanding of how pasta and noodles can be paired with whichever savory ingredients taste best to you. In this way, the recipes in this chapter serve to complete my demonstration of how versatile pasta and noodles can be.

Understanding Pasta Ingredients

It doesn't take many ingredients to make pasta. A well-stocked pantry and refrigerator, combined with a short shopping list, are all you need to make many enticing dishes: all-purpose flour, eggs, and olive oil for making the dough, plus butter, milk or cream, fresh or canned tomatoes, onions, garlic, and fresh and dried herbs for the sauces. Be sure to select high-quality ingredients to give your pastas the superior flavor such simplicity requires.

Dough Ingredients

Pasta doughs are made from basic ingredients. Most recipes begin with unbleached all-purpose (plain) flour—the versatile flour that's probably in a canister in your kitchen right now. Milled from a blend of high- and low-gluten wheat, it is suitable for all kinds of recipes. Using unbleached flour gives pasta dough a slightly creamy color and a better flavor than bleached flour. Gluten is the protein in wheat that provides pasta with the strength and

elasticity necessary to roll, stretch, and cook the dough without its breaking apart. Gluten-rich semolina flour, milled from durum wheat, is used for dough made into intricate shapes, such as orecchiette and *cavatelli*, and for quality dried pasta. Buckwheat, used for Japanese soba noodles, is neither a type of wheat nor a cereal grain but the seed of an herb. Flour made from buckwheat has more starch and less protein than wheat flour, so it is used along with all-purpose flour, which contributes structure.

Be sure the eggs you use for pasta are fresh; they provide golden color, subtle flavor, and additional protein. In this book, large eggs are specified. Using larger or smaller ones will alter the proportions of the recipes. Choose extra-virgin olive oil for pasta dough for its flavor and purity. Store it away from light and heat to preserve freshness.

Sauce Ingredients

You'll regularly use fresh plum (Roma) tomatoes for quick-cooking and long-

simmered sauces. Garlic lends a heady accent, while onions deliver a mildly sweet foundation to both meat sauces and all-vegetable recipes such as Classic Tomato Sauce (page 92). Carrots and celery are indispensable when you make a *soffrito*, the starting point for Bolognese Sauce (page 49). Shallots, small members of the onion family, add their subtle flavor to such dishes as Fettuccine with Shrimp, Tomato & Cream (page 61). When making a creamy sauce, it's best to use rich heavy (double) cream, which can be boiled without separating and smoothly coats fettuccine or other fresh pasta. European-style unsalted butter also lends a wonderful richness.

Filling Ingredients

Fillings for tortellini or ravioli must include a perfect balance of moist and dry ingredients so that the mixtures cling together but are not sticky. Typically that means combining sausage or ground (minced) beef or chicken with eggs and/or fine dried bread crumbs. Ricotta and mozzarella cheeses play prominent roles in many fillings, while mascarpone, an Italian double- or triple-cream cheese, adds a special richness to cheese fillings. For Asian pot stickers, common ingredients are ground pork or shellfish, green (spring) onions, napa cabbage, shiitake mushrooms, and fresh ginger.

Pantry Ingredients

One of the advantages of mastering pasta is that it enables you to create an impressive dish at a moment's notice. What makes that possible is that you can have most of what you need on hand in your pantry at all times.

Seek out some of the many varieties of high-quality dried pastas and Asian noodles available, which are the foundation of many traditional pasta dishes. Extra-virgin olive oil is indispensable in recipes where you'll taste its flavor. Oil labeled simply "olive oil" can be used for cooking meats and and other strongly flavored ingredients. Soy sauce, often used in dipping sauces for Asian noodles, is another ingredient you'll use regularly. Dried herbs, such as bay leaves, rosemary, and oregano, turn up in many recipes. They lose their flavor after several months, so restock regularly. Have premium canned peeled tomatoes on hand; I always use imported varieties labeled "Italian peeled tomatoes." Keep a wedge of Parmigiano-Reggiano cheese in the refrigerator, ready to grate as needed for fillings or to pass at the table.

Cooking & Seasoning Pasta

Scan a restaurant menu and the names of favorite foods seem to leap out, evoking taste memories. As you learn to cook, something similar happens. Read a recipe carefully and you begin to imagine the resulting flavors. At the same time, you start to learn to trust your instincts about how to heighten flavors by adding a touch more of something, as well as whether to cook something a little longer or to serve it *right now!*

Timing

When cooking pasta, timing is everything. Experienced cooks seem to know instinctively how to dovetail cooking tasks so that all the components of a dish come together simultaneously.

You can sense how this happens by noting how ingredients are specified in recipe lists. If an onion needs to be chopped or a cheese grated, have these foods prepped before you begin cooking. The recipe methods in this book use numbered steps, so that you can easily follow them to produce a finished dish with each element perfectly cooked.

Since most pasta preparations consist of cooked pasta plus some sort of sauce, you'll want both ready to combine and serve at once. Time this correctly and the two parts will come together in one delicious whole.

You may begin some dishes well in advance of serving. The White Sauce (page 28) at the heart of Spinach Lasagna (page 81) can be made a couple days ahead, refrigerated, and reheated when you assemble the dish. The beef filling for Ravioli (page 67) or Tortellini (page 75) can be refrigerated overnight.

Cooking Pasta

You may have heard old wives' tales about cooking pasta. It's necessary to separate them from the genuinely useful tips in this book. For example, forget about adding olive oil to the boiling water in which pasta cooks. It does not prevent pasta from sticking together. Indeed, most of the oil floats to the surface, so you are only wasting oil.

Stated simply, the best way to cook any pasta is in a big pot in a lot of water. Pasta tends to clump up if it lacks room to swirl about during cooking. For a pound (500 g) of pasta, fill a large pot about three-fourths full of water (about 5 quarts/5 liters), bring the water to a rolling boil, and salt it generously.

Add the pasta all at once. For dried pasta, push it gently below the surface of the water to soften it quickly. After the water returns to a boil, stir to separate the pasta and to keep it from sticking to the pan, and continue to stir occasionally. Filled pastas such as ravioli also need plenty of water for cooking. After adding them, adjust the heat so the water barely simmers to keep them from breaking.

Pour cooked pasta into a colander to drain, saving some of the water to use for adjusting the consistency of the accompanying sauce. Shake the pasta briefly to remove excess water, but leave a little clinging to the pasta. This moisture helps to unite the pasta and the sauce.

Food Safety

When draining cooked pasta, wear thick oven mitts and tip the cooking pan away from you as you pour the pasta into the colander. This keeps you from spilling any boiling water onto yourself and prevents steam rising from the water and pasta from burning your hands and arms.

Don't rinse pasta unless it's indicated in the recipe; rinsing cools it needlessly and makes it sticky.

Al dente—"to the tooth"—is the Italian term for perfectly cooked pasta. In other words, it should retain some resistance to the bite. Cook fresh pasta only until tender but still slightly chewy; cook dried pasta until a thin white line shows at the center when you bite into it. For more on cooking pasta, turn to pages 36–38.

Seasoning Pasta

The principal seasoning for pasta, added to the cooking water once it boils, is kosher salt or sea salt (favored by many cooks for their superior flavor). The amount of salt—about 2 tablespoons for 5 quarts (5 liters) of water—may seem like a lot, but it achieves a level important to Italian cooks: water as salty as the sea.

Seasoning Fillings

How can you know if a raw meat or seafood pasta filling is seasoned just right? Sampling raw ingredients is not only misleading (cooking transforms many flavors) but may also be unsafe. Instead, spoon out a nugget of the uncooked mixture and cook it briefly in a small frying pan. Let it cool slightly, then taste critically. Add salt or other seasonings to the main mixture to taste, keeping in mind that the flavors of the filling should balance those in the sauce.

Seasoning Sauces

Many pasta sauces are surprisingly simple, so fresh, high-quality seasonings are essential to their success. Make a habit of grating whole nutmeg and grinding peppercorns as needed, and grating Parmigiano-Reggiano cheese just before serving. Use the seasoning amounts in the recipes as guidelines, but always keep extra on hand so you can adjust the flavors to your liking. When cooking, start with small amounts of salt and other seasonings, taste, and then add more as needed. If a dish will be finished with a dusting of cheese, undersalt the sauce slightly, as the cheese will add to the overall saltiness of the dish.

Food Safety

To keep bacteria on the surface of raw meat from spreading to other ingredients, reserve one cutting board for meats and another for vegetables. Wash all your tools with hot, soapy water after each use, as well.

Serving Pasta

You've worked hard and now comes your reward—feasting on your carefully crafted pasta and sauce. Remember these easy principles: as the pasta finishes cooking, check the consistency of the sauce to be sure it's neither too thick nor too thin; work quickly to drain the pasta and mix it with the hot sauce; and finally, the sooner the dish is served, the better it will taste. Pasta should always arrive at the table steaming hot.

Saucing Pasta

Combining pasta and sauce successfully depends on draining the pasta promptly after cooking, but leaving the strands moist. Save a little of the cooking water in case it's needed to thin the sauce. This water contains a little starch and is better than plain water, which could make your sauce too thin. A sauce that is too thick will be difficult to distribute evenly throughout, and one that is too thin will sit in a pool beneath the pasta, rather than thoroughly coating each piece.

Many Italians believe Americans use too much sauce when making pasta. Try to refrain from oversaucing; you should be able to enjoy the flavor of both the pasta and the sauce in every bite. Keep in mind that fresh pasta is more absorbent than dried, so it may take a bit more sauce.

Serving Dishes

Warming serving dishes will help to keep pasta temptingly hot. Place plates, bowls, and/or platters in a 200°F (95°C) oven for about 15 minutes. Wear oven mitts when you serve the pasta. And caution diners that the plates will be hot.

Garnishes

Serving pasta with panache is simple: dust freshly grated nutmeg over creamy fettuccine or sprinkle thinly sliced green onions over Pad Thai (page 126). Throughout this book, you'll find other finishing touches, among them grated cheese, chopped fresh herbs, or a drizzle of white truffle oil. Such garnishes contribute style, color, and flavor.

Measuring Ingredients

While some noted cooks appear to have a nonchalant attitude about measurements, the "I'll just add a little bit of cream" school of cooking is ill suited to the inexperienced. Indeed, this kitchen style is a formula for disaster unless it's based on long practice. Until you've cooked enough to have developed a reliable sense of quantities, you will achieve much better results by using the standard measurements found in the recipes that follow.

Mise en Place

An important rule of cooking is to begin by assembling everything the task requires. French-trained chefs call this practice *mise en place*, or "setting in place." In other words, all the recipe ingredients and the tools and utensils required to cook them should be at hand.

To find out what you'll need, read the recipe from start to finish. If a dish is cooked in several lengthy stages, note when you'll have time to prepare for the next step. For a quick-cooking dish, conversely, it's important to have every element prepped and ready to go when you begin. Many of the master recipes that follow include *mise en place* among the steps, an illustration of its importance.

Always begin your *mise en place* by thoroughly rinsing all the produce you will need. Recipes do not usually include rinsing instructions. Then read the ingredients list again carefully. It alerts you to items that need to be prepared—peeled, chopped, sliced—before measuring. Prepare and measure them in advance and be sure to use the proper measuring equipment.

Liquid Ingredients

Measuring cups for liquids are made of clear, heatproof glass or plastic and have a pouring spout. On one side, markings indicate fractions of a cup and fluid ounces. Most cups are also calibrated on the opposite side in milliliters. For accuracy, place the cup on a flat surface to read the measure at eye level.

Dry Ingredients

Flour, dried herbs, bread crumbs, grated cheese—all are included in the category of dry ingredients. They require another kind of measuring cup, one in which the ingredients can be leveled off. Made of metal (stainless steel or aluminum) or plastic, they are usually sold in sets that measure amounts from ¼ cup to 1 cup.

When you measure flour, use the spoon-and-sweep method: spoon flour into the measuring cup loosely, then level off the top with the straight edge of a knife. Some "puffy" ingredients, such as minced herbs or shredded cheese, require packing them lightly into the cup for measuring.

Measuring Spoons

Use measuring spoons for all ingredients expressed in teaspoons or tablespoons. Most sets include 4 spoons, ranging from ¼ teaspoon to 1 tablespoon. To use the spoons for dry measures, scoop up the ingredient and then level the top with a straight edge. For liquid ingredients, fill the spoons to the rim.

Pairing Pasta & Sauce

Linguine with clam sauce, fettuccine Bolognese—some pasta combinations are classic. What makes one pasta a better choice than another for baking under a blanket of cheese or piling on a platter with a meaty tomato sauce? The rudiments of matching pasta and sauce have long been known in Italy. But you don't always need to adhere to tradition. Follow these guidelines and you will soon be creating your own dishes.

EXAMPLES

fettuccine
Wide ribbons.

lasagna
Large, wide strips; typically layered with sauces and baked.

pappardelle
Very wide ribbons.

tagliatelle
Slightly wider ribbons than fettuccine.

SUGGESTED SAUCES

Alfredo (page 55): Rich, luxurious sauce made with cream, butter, and Parmigiano-Reggiano cheese.

Bolognese (page 49): Long-simmered, chunky tomato-and-meat sauce.

Butter & Sage (page 61): Butter-based sauce with Parmigiano-Reggiano cheese.

Cream Sauce Variations (pages 60–61): Cream-based sauces that feature complementary ingredients, from fresh spring vegetables or earthy mushrooms to pungent Gorgonzola cheese.

Tomato Cream (page 94): Smooth tomato sauce enriched with cream.

PAIRING GUIDELINES

Long pastas made with fresh eggs and all-purpose flour are more tender and absorbent than other kinds of pasta. They also have a more delicate flavor. Pair them with thick, creamy sauces, which nicely coat the silky ribbons and won't overpower their subtlety.

Long, fresh pastas are also good with lightly textured sauces. The long, often wide noodles easily wrap around bits of meat and vegetables.

Be careful when pairing fresh pastas made with spices or vegetable purées; they can clash with sauce flavors.

EXAMPLES

cavatelli
Narrow football shape, tapered at the ends.

orecchiette
Small, indented circular shape.

SUGGESTED SAUCES

Broccoli Rabe & Sausage (page 63): Hearty olive oil–based sauce with sautéed greens and sausage.

Fresh Tomatoes & Mozzarella (page 65): Uncooked tomato sauce tossed with cubes of fresh mozzarella cheese.

PAIRING GUIDELINES

Fresh shaped pastas can be made from a sturdy semolina flour–based pasta dough, or can be purchased dried. They pair well with substantial, chunky sauces, since the bits of meat and vegetables nestle easily inside the openings.

EXAMPLES

ravioli
Stuffed fresh squares or rounds.

tortellini
Small, stuffed rounds.

SUGGESTED SAUCES

Classic Tomato (page 92) or **Tomato Cream** (page 94): Smooth *soffrito*-based tomato sauce; can be enriched with cream.

Butter & Sage (page 61): Butter-based sauce with Parmigiano-Reggiano cheese.

PAIRING GUIDELINES

Consider the filling when picking the sauce: the more strongly flavored the filling, the more robust the sauce should be.

EXAMPLES

bucatini/perciatelli
Narrow tubes; traditional match for *amatriciana* sauce.

capellini
Very thin, delicate strands. Also known as angel hair.

fedelini
Strands, thinner than spaghetti.

linguine
Flat, narrow ribbons; a traditional match for *aglio olio* sauce and clam sauce.

spaghetti
Thin cylindrical strands; a traditional match for carbonara sauce.

vermicelli
Slender form of spaghetti.

SUGGESTED SAUCES

Aglio Olio (page 97): Spicy olive oil–based sauce with garlic and parsley.

Amatriciana (page 95): Robust tomato sauce with diced pancetta.

Arrabbiata (page 95): Spicy, smooth tomato sauce.

Carbonara (page 102): Made from eggs, pancetta, and *pecorino romano* cheese.

Clam (page 99): Olive oil–based sauce with clams, garlic, and parsley.

Classic Tomato (page 92): Smooth tomato sauce based on sautéed onions and other vegetables.

Marinara (page 94): Assertive tomato sauce based on olive oil and garlic.

Puttanesca (page 95): Slightly chunky tomato sauce with olives and capers.

PAIRING GUIDELINES

Long dried pastas pair well with smooth sauces that coat the strands evenly.

Dried pastas go especially well with olive oil–based sauces. The oil clings readily to the naturally rough surface of the pasta, coating their length.

They also match well with sauces that have slightly chunky ingredients (olives or diced pancetta), which are easily trapped in the twirled strands. Avoid sauces with very large chunks, or the chunks will be left in the bottom of the bowl.

Reserve more delicate strand pastas, such as capellini or vermicelli, for light, smooth, simple sauces.

EXAMPLES

conchiglie
Small or large shell shape.

farfalle
Bow-tie shape.

fusilli
Corkscrew-shaped tubes.

macaroni
Small curved tubes.

penne
Narrow tubes with angled ends.

SUGGESTED SAUCES

Arrabbiata (page 95): Spicy, smooth tomato sauce.

Cheese Sauce (page 106): Creamy white sauce mixed with sharp Cheddar cheese.

Marinara (page 94): Assertive tomato sauce based on olive oil and garlic.

Mushrooms, Garlic & Parsley (page 99): Olive oil–based sauce with slices of fresh mushrooms and herbs.

Pesto, Potatoes & Green Beans (page 101): Robust, olive oil–based, puréed herb sauce with chunky vegetables.

PAIRING GUIDELINES

Short dried pasta shapes are very versatile. Any shape pairs well with tomato sauce. Match macaroni with a creamy cheese sauce. Toss corkscrews or butterflies with a chunky sauce. The chunks will lodge in the twists and hollows. And since shaped pasta is chunky itself, both the pasta and ingredients are easy to pick up in one bite.

These pastas are also good match for olive oil–based sauces. Their rough texture, from the semolina flour, offers a surface to which these sauces can cling.

EXAMPLE

gnocchi
Tender, bite-sized dumplings made from riced potatoes.

SUGGESTED SAUCES

Alfredo (page 55): Creamy, rich sauce with Parmigiano-Reggiano cheese.

Pesto (page 101) or **Amatriciana** (page 95): Robust, olive oil–based, puréed herb or tomato sauce.

PAIRING GUIDELINES

Dumplings have enough body to stand up to smooth, tomato-based sauces or puréed herb sauces. They also pair well with creamy sauces.

1

Basic Recipes

Making pasta at home can be a pleasurable and rewarding experience, and the resulting flavor is better than almost any "fresh" pastas you can buy. You'll see on the following pages how easy it is to make the dough in a food processor. Try both tender egg pasta, with or without spinach, and a stiffer egg-free dough for forming into shapes. A white sauce is also included for use in many pasta recipes.

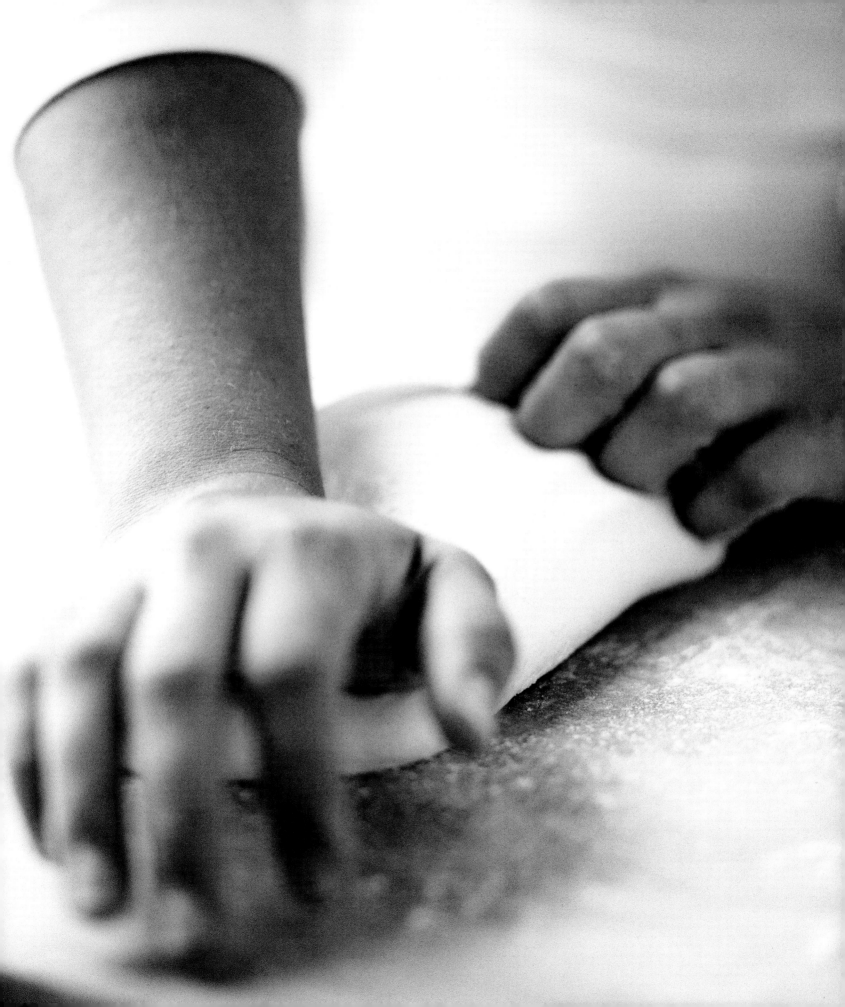

Fresh Egg Pasta Dough

Fresh pasta enriched with eggs forms a delicate foundation for a variety of dishes. A food processor makes quick work of mixing the flour, eggs, and oil into a soft dough before you knead it into a smooth, silky mass. The processor saves you time over the traditional hand method, and the result is just as good.

2½ cups (12½ oz/390 g) unbleached all-purpose (plain) flour, plus extra for dusting

4 large eggs

2 teaspoons extra-virgin olive oil

MAKES ABOUT 1 LB (500 G)

CHEF'S TIP
You can flavor this dough with 1 tablespoon of a crumbled dried herb, such as marjoram or thyme, or 1 teaspoon freshly and finely ground black pepper. Add either seasoning to the work bowl with the flour.

1 **Add the flour to a food processor**
Fit a food processor with the metal blade. Add 2 cups (10 oz/315 g) of the flour to the food processor work bowl. Set the remaining ½ cup (2½ oz/75 g) flour nearby; you'll use it later to adjust the consistency of the dough.

2 **Add the eggs and oil**
Crack the side of 1 egg sharply on a flat surface rather than on the rim of a bowl. (This will reduce shell fragments.) Drop the egg into a small glass measuring cup. Repeat with the remaining eggs, then check the cup carefully to make sure the eggs are free of shell bits. Add the olive oil to the measuring cup. (Many traditional Italian recipes for fresh pasta do not include olive oil, but I like to add it to make the dough softer and more manageable.) Pour the egg-oil mixture into the processor.

3 **Mix the dough**
Process the mixture until the flour is evenly moistened and crumbly; this will take about 10 seconds. If the dough seems excessively sticky, add some of the reserved flour 1 tablespoon at a time, processing until the flour is incorporated; you may not need all of it. Try not to add more flour than is necessary, or the dough could turn out stiff and dry. Each time you stop the machine, pinch the dough between your fingers. It should feel a little firmer each time. After about 30 seconds of processing, the dough should come together and form a loose ball on top of the blade, and feel moist but not sticky when pinched.

4   Prepare the work surface

Dust a wood or slightly rough plastic work surface with all-purpose flour. Either surface will grip the finished dough better than a smooth surface, making kneading the dough easier. Remove the ball of dough from the food processor and place it in the center of the floured surface.

5   Lightly knead the dough

With the heel of one hand, push the ball of dough away from you. Lift it from the far side with your fingers, fold it back toward you, and then rotate the dough a quarter turn. Again, push the dough away with the heel of one hand, pull it back with your fingertips, and rotate a quarter turn. Stop kneading the dough when it feels damp without being sticky and is an even yellow with no streaks of flour. This will take only a minute or two. You will continue kneading with the pasta machine later.

6   Let the dough rest

Shape the dough into a ball. It will be quite elastic at this point and would spring back on itself if you attempted to roll it out. Cover the ball with a large overturned bowl and let it rest for 30 minutes. During this time the gluten in the flour will relax, making it easier to roll out the dough into a thin, delicate, but strong sheet.

CHEF'S TIP

You can reduce the quantities of this recipe to make just enough for 1 large or 2 small servings—the perfect quantity for a quick weeknight meal or for practicing rolling out and cutting strands. Use ⅔ cup (3½ oz/105 g) plus 1 tablespoon unbleached all-purpose (plain) flour and 1 large egg. (You can omit the olive oil.)

RECOMMENDED USES
Use this dough for fettuccine, ravioli, tortellini, and lasagna.

Fresh Spinach Pasta Dough

Fresh spinach not only turns egg pasta dough a beautiful grass green, but also imparts a subtle flavor that pairs well with robust sauces. The finished spinach dough is softer and easier to manipulate than plain egg pasta and has a creamier, more delicate texture when cooked.

1 bunch spinach, about 10 oz (315 g)

¼ cup (2 fl oz/60 ml) water

3 large eggs

2½ cups (12½ oz/390 g) unbleached all-purpose (plain) flour, plus extra for dusting

MAKES ABOUT 18 OZ (560 G)

1 Stem and rinse the spinach

Sort through the spinach, discarding any yellowed or wilted leaves. Gently fold each of the remaining leaves in half along the stem, with the vein side facing out. Grasp the stem with your other hand and quickly tear it away to remove the coarse, tough part of the vein. Fill a large bowl with cool water, immerse the leaves in the water, and use a swishing motion to loosen any sand and grit from the leaves, which will fall to the bottom of the bowl. Rinse the leaves at least twice more in clean water until there is no sand or grit visible in the bottom of the bowl. Shake the spinach lightly and place it in a large colander to drain.

2 Cook and drain the spinach

In a large pot over medium heat, combine the rinsed spinach and the ¼ cup water. Cover the pot and cook the spinach, uncovering the pot to stir now and again with a wooden spoon, until wilted and tender, 4–5 minutes. The water in the leaves is forced out during cooking, reducing the volume of the spinach dramatically. Drain the spinach in a colander, pushing down with the spoon to release as much water as possible, and then let the spinach cool slightly. Place the spinach in a lint-free kitchen towel and wring it as dry as possible (excess moisture in the spinach will cause the dough to be too loose). You should have about ½ cup (3½ oz/105 g) packed cooked spinach.

3 Process the spinach and eggs

Fit a food processor with the metal blade. Add the spinach to the food processor work bowl. Break the eggs into a small glass measuring cup and check carefully to make sure they are free of shell bits. Pour the eggs into the processor with the spinach and process until the mixture is smooth and well blended.

4 Add the flour and mix the dough

Add 2 cups (10 oz/315 g) of the flour to the food processor. Set the remaining ½ cup (2½ oz/75 g) flour nearby; you'll use it later to adjust the consistency of the dough. Process the mixture until the flour is evenly moistened and crumbly; this will take about 10 seconds. If the dough seems excessively sticky, add some of the reserved flour 1 tablespoon at a time, processing until the flour is incorporated; you may not need all of it. Try not to add more flour than is necessary, or the dough could turn out stiff and dry. Each time you stop the machine, pinch the dough between your fingers. It should feel a little firmer each time. After about 30 seconds of processing, the dough should come together and form a loose ball on top of the blade, and feel moist but not sticky when pinched.

5 Prepare the work surface

Dust a wood or slightly rough plastic work surface with all-purpose flour. Either surface will grip the finished dough better than a smooth surface, making kneading the dough easier. Remove the ball of dough from the food processor and place it in the center of the floured surface.

6 Knead the dough

With the heel of one hand, push the ball of dough away from you. Lift it from the far side with your fingers, fold it back toward you, and then rotate the dough a quarter turn. Again, push the dough away with the heel of one hand, pull it back with your fingertips, and rotate a quarter turn. Stop kneading the dough when it feels damp without being sticky and is an even green with no streaks of flour. This will take only a minute or two. You will continue kneading with the pasta machine later.

7 Let the dough rest

Shape the dough into a ball. It will be quite elastic at this point and would spring back on itself if you attempted to roll it out. Cover the ball with a large overturned bowl and let it rest for 30 minutes. During this time the gluten in the flour will relax, making it easier to roll out the dough into a thin, delicate, but strong sheet.

CHEF'S TIP

Keep in mind that the amount of flour the dough will absorb varies according to the flour, the freshness of the eggs, and the weather. You may need a bit more flour on a rainy day and a little less on a hot, dry day.

RECOMMENDED USES

Use this dough for fettuccine, ravioli, tortellini, and lasagna.

Fresh Semolina Pasta Dough

In this recipe, golden semolina flour, with the texture of fine sand, is combined with all-purpose flour and water, but no eggs. The result is a stiff dough that is used to make short, shaped pastas. Like the other pasta doughs in this chapter, semolina dough is easy to mix, but it will be more difficult to knead.

2 cups (10 oz/315 g) unbleached all-purpose (plain) flour, plus extra for dusting

¾ cup (4 oz/125 g) finely ground semolina flour (do not substitute coarsely ground)

1 teaspoon kosher salt

¾ cup (6 fl oz/180 ml) warm water, or as needed

MAKES ABOUT 1 LB (500 G)

1 Combine the dry ingredients
Fit a food processor with the metal blade. Add the all-purpose and semolina flours and the salt to the food processor work bowl. Pulse the machine a few times to mix the ingredients.

2 Test the water
Turn on the hot water tap and let it run for a while to warm the water. Using a glass measuring cup, measure ¾ cup of the warm tap water, then use an instant-read thermometer to check the temperature; it should register 105°F (40°C). Warming the water helps to activate the gluten in the flour and contributes to a stiff, but pliable dough.

3 Mix the dough
With the food processor running, pour ½ cup (4 fl oz/125 ml) of the warm water through the feed tube in a thin, steady stream. You want to add just enough water to moisten the dough. If necessary, add the remaining water 1 tablespoon at a time; you may not need all of it. After about 30 seconds of processing, the dough should come together and form a loose ball on top of the blade. Remove the top of the food processor and pinch the dough to check its texture; it should feel moist but not sticky. If the dough seems too dry, add a teaspoon of water and process until blended. Do not add more water than is necessary, or the dough will be too soft to shape.

4 Prepare the work surface

Dust a wood or slightly rough plastic work surface with all-purpose flour. Either surface will grip the finished dough better than a smooth surface, making kneading—and later, rolling and shaping—the dough easier. Remove the ball of dough from the food processor and place it in the center of the floured surface.

5 Knead the dough

With the heel of one hand, push the ball of dough away from you. Lift it from the far side with your fingers, fold it back toward you, and then rotate the dough a quarter turn. Again, push the dough away with the heel of one hand, pull it back with your fingertips, and rotate a quarter turn. Because there are no eggs or oil in this dough and it calls for harder semolina flour, the dough will be more difficult to work with than fresh egg pasta dough. Also, semolina flour is higher in protein than all-purpose flour, resulting in a more complex gluten network. Stop kneading the dough when it is smooth and feels damp without being sticky. This will take only a minute or two. (Unlike fresh egg pasta dough, you don't need to knead the dough further with a pasta machine.)

6 Let the dough rest

Shape the dough into a ball. It will be quite elastic at this point and would spring back on itself if you attempted to work with it. Cover the ball with a large overturned bowl and let it rest for 30 minutes. During this time the gluten in the flour will relax, making it easier to shape the dough.

CHEF'S TIP

Covering the pasta with an overturned bowl is a simple and environmentally sound way of keeping the dough from drying out as it rests. The alternative is to use plastic wrap.

RECOMMENDED USES

Use this dough for orecchiette, cavatelli, or other shaped pastas.

White Sauce

Wonderfully rich, this versatile sauce, similar to the French béchamel sauce, carries the flavors of fresh butter and milk. When Cheddar cheese is added, it becomes a sauce for macaroni and cheese (page 106). On its own, white sauce is often a traditional element of lasagna (page 81) or Gnocchi Gratin (page 111).

2 cups (16 fl oz/500 ml) whole milk

4 tablespoons (2 oz/60 g) unsalted butter

¼ cup (1½ oz/45 g) all-purpose (plain) flour

½ teaspoon kosher salt

MAKES ABOUT 2 CUPS (16 FL OZ/500 ML)

1 **Heat the milk**
In a small nonreactive saucepan over medium heat, warm the milk just until small bubbles appear along the edges of the pan, about 5 minutes. During this time, watch the milk carefully and adjust the heat under the burner if necessary. Don't let the milk to come to a boil; this causes a skin to form and will affect the texture of the sauce. Remove the pan from the heat and cover to keep warm.

2 **Cook the butter and flour**
Place a heavy-bottomed nonreactive saucepan over medium-low heat and add the butter. When the butter has melted, add the flour and stir well with a wooden spoon. At first the mixture will look lumpy, but continue to stir and adjust the heat as necessary to keep the mixture gently bubbling until the mixture is pale and ivory. (This slow cooking is important because it helps the sauce thicken to the correct degree when the milk is added later.) After 2–3 minutes, the mixture will have come together in a thick, smooth paste, which is known as a *roux*. Remove the pan from the heat.

3 **Incorporate the milk into the roux**
With the pan still off the heat, begin stirring with a whisk as you slowly drizzle a tablespoon or two of the hot milk into the roux. The mixture will immediately become thick and lumpy. While whisking constantly, continue adding the milk about 2 tablespoons at a time. The sauce will gradually become smooth. After about ½ cup (4 fl oz/125 ml) of the milk has been added, you can start to add the rest a little more rapidly. As you stir, be sure you to run the whisk along the bottom of the pan, covering the entire surface to the sides. This will ensure that all the roux has been incorporated into the sauce.

4 Cook the sauce

When all of the milk has been added, the sauce should have the consistency of thick cream. At this point, switch back to the wooden spoon and stir in the salt. Place the saucepan over medium heat and cook, stirring constantly, until small bubbles just begin breaking on the surface and the sauce is smooth and thick enough to coat the back of the spoon, about 1 minute longer. Adjust the heat, if necessary, to keep the sauce at this gentle simmer; if the heat is too high, it can scorch and ruin your sauce.

5 Evaluate the sauce

Taste the sauce; it should taste creamy and neutral, with no trace of raw flour flavor. You don't want to season the sauce further at this point, as it will be combined with other ingredients later. If, despite your careful stirring, lumps are still visible in the sauce, pour it through a fine-mesh sieve into a bowl.

6 Use or store the sauce

Use the sauce right away, or store it. To store, transfer the hot sauce to a bowl (if you haven't already) and cover it with a piece of plastic wrap, pressing the wrap directly onto the surface of the sauce to prevent a skin from forming. Let the sauce cool slightly (this should take about 10 minutes), then store it in the refrigerator for up to 2 days. To reheat refrigerated white sauce, pour it into a heavy-bottomed saucepan, place over low heat, and stir constantly with a wooden spoon or whisk, adding a little hot water or milk to thin it, if necessary.

CHEF'S TIP

It is important to run the whisk over the bottom of the pan to incorporate all the roux into the milk. Some people refer to the process as "getting into the corners of the pan," even though round saucepans have no true corners.

RECOMMENDED USES

Use this sauce for lasagna, macaroni and cheese, gnocchi gratin, and other baked pasta dishes.

2

Key Techniques

Once you've mastered making fresh pasta dough, you will be ready for rolling, cutting, and shaping it into an array of sizes and shapes. In this chapter, these skills are clearly explained. You will also learn how to cook fresh, dried, and filled pasta perfectly, and how to handle several common ingredients used in making pasta sauces, including garlic, tomatoes, and fresh herbs.

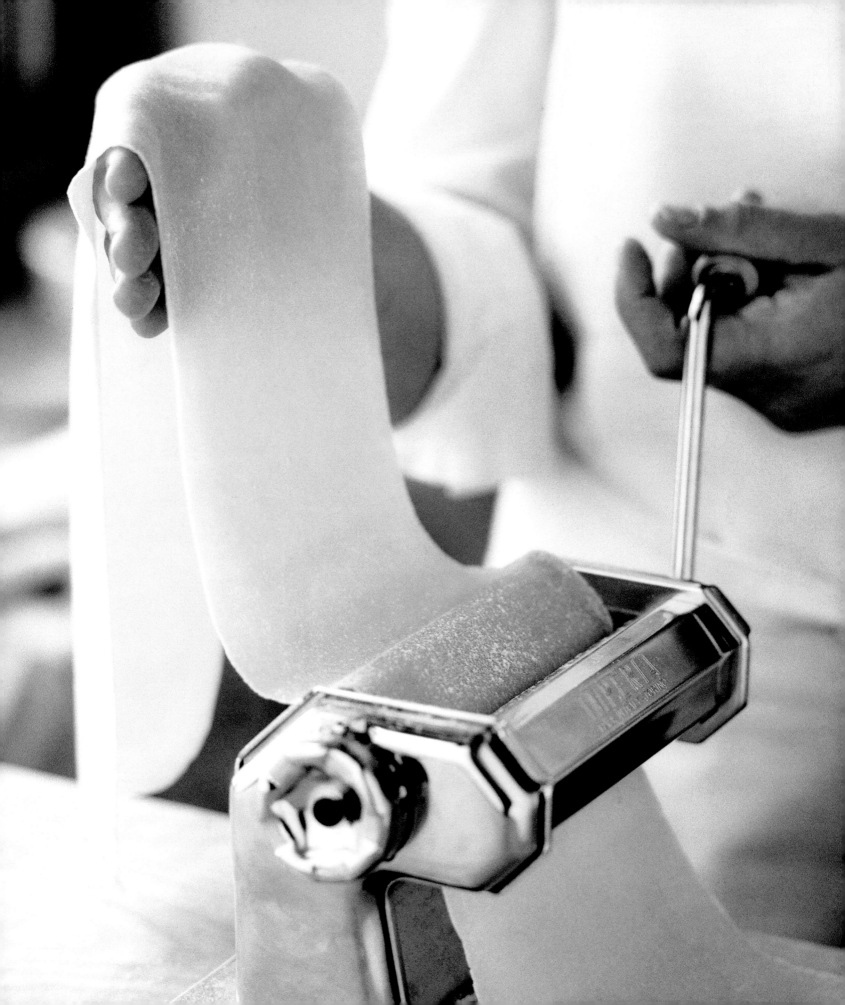

Kneading & Rolling Out Fresh Pasta Dough

1 Set up the pasta machine
Follow the manufacturer's instructions to anchor the machine to the counter, usually with a vicelike tool. Turn the dial to set the rollers at the widest setting. Attach the crank.

2 Dust the rollers with flour
Lightly dust the rollers with flour so the pasta won't stick as you run it through the machine. If at any time during the rolling process the dough feels sticky, flour the rollers again.

3 Flatten the dough into a disk
Use a bench scraper or chef's knife to cut the dough into 4 pieces; slip 3 pieces back under the bowl. Flatten the remaining piece into a disk ½ inch (12 mm) thick.

5 Roll out the dough
Move the dial to the next notch to narrow the rollers and pass the dough through again, catching the longer, thinner end with your hand and easing it onto the work surface.

TROUBLESHOOTING
Pasta dough can stick or tear in the machine if it is too moist, or if a scrap of dough gets caught in the rollers. To fix this, fold up the dough neatly, flour it well, and start the rolling process over again at step 5.

6 Continue rolling out the dough
Continue passing the dough through progressively narrower rollers until you reach the second-to-last setting. As you work, keep adjusting the dough on the work surface so it lays flat.

4 Knead the dough

Turn the crank to pass the disk through the rollers. Fold the dough into thirds like a letter, dust 1 side with flour, and roll again. Repeat 8–10 times until smooth and satiny.

Cutting Fresh Pasta Dough

1 Cut the pasta into sections

Cut the dough into sections as directed in the recipe. For fettuccine or lasagna, let the sections dry for 10–20 minutes, turning them once or twice. For filled pastas, use the dough right away.

2 Secure the cutting attachment

Follow the manufacturer's instructions to put the strand-cutting attachment you need onto the pasta machine. (On some machines, two strand widths are on the same attachment.)

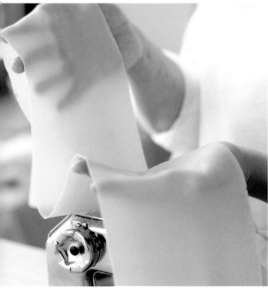

7 Test for thinness

Hold the dough in your hands: If you can see your hand through it, the dough is ready (it should be about 1/16 inch/2 mm thick). If necessary, pass it through the narrowest setting.

3 Cut the pasta into strands

Attach the crank to the blades. One at a time, insert the dough sections into the blades and turn the crank to create strands. Ease them onto the work surface with your free hand.

4 Let the strands dry

Spread the strands out on a lightly floured baking sheet, separating them so they have room, and let them dry for 10–20 minutes. They should feel slightly leathery, but not be brittle.

Shaping Orecchiette

1 Divide the dough
Lightly dust your work surface with flour. Using a bench scraper or chef's knife, cut the dough into 4 equal pieces. Shape each piece of dough into a short cylinder.

2 Roll the dough into logs
Place the fingers of both hands on one of the dough cylinders and roll it back and forth, gradually shifting your hands to the ends, to form a log about ½ inch (12 mm) in diameter.

3 Cut the logs into pieces
Again using the bench scraper or knife, cut each rolled-out log into ½-inch (12-mm) pieces. The pieces will look like tiny pillows.

4 Form a dough piece into a disk
Extend your index finger along the blade of a table knife. With the tip of the knife, flatten a piece of dough and drag it slightly toward you over the work surface to form a disk.

5 Press the disk over your thumb
Gently push the disk over the tip of your thumb to form a small cup. Repeat steps 4 and 5 to shape the remaining pieces.

6 Let the orecchiette dry
As you work, spread the orecchiette out on a lightly floured rimmed baking sheet (don't let the pieces touch, or they might stick together). Cook them right away or let dry for up to 2 hours.

Shaping Cavatelli

1 Divide the dough
Lightly dust your work surface with flour. Using a chef's knife or bench scraper, cut the dough into 4 equal pieces. Shape each piece of dough into a short cylinder.

2 Roll the dough into logs
Place the fingers of both hands on one of the dough cylinders and roll it back and forth, gradually shifting your hands to the ends, to form a log about ½ inch (12 mm) in diameter.

3 Cut the logs into pieces
Again using the knife or bench scraper, cut each rolled-out log into ½-inch (12-mm) pieces. The pieces will look like tiny pillows.

4 Flatten a piece of dough
Turn a dough piece so a cut side faces up. Extend your index finger along the blade of a table knife. Hold the blade horizontally above one of the pieces and press down to flatten it.

5 Curl the dough around the knife
Drag the knife gently to one side as you press down on the dough. The dough will curl around the knife into an oblong pasta shell. Repeat steps 4 and 5 to shape the remaining pieces.

6 Let the *cavatelli* dry
As you work, spread the *cavatelli* out on a lightly floured rimmed baking sheet (don't let the pieces touch, or they might stick together). Cook them right away or let dry for up to 2 hours.

Cooking Fresh Pasta

1 Salt the boiling water
Bring a large pot three-fourths full of water to a rolling boil. You'll need about 5 qt (5 l) of water to cook 1 lb (500 g) of pasta. Add about 2 tablespoons kosher salt to the water.

2 Add the pasta to the water
Add the fresh pasta to the boiling water all at once. Since fresh pasta cooks so quickly, it's important to make sure all the pasta is added at the same time.

3 Stir the pasta
Using a wooden spoon, gently stir the pasta occasionally to prevent it from sticking together. Adjust the heat if needed to keep the water at a boil, but don't let it boil over.

4 Test the pasta for doneness
After 1½ minutes, remove a strand from the pot, let it cool slightly, and taste it. It should be tender but still slightly chewy. If not, continue to cook for several seconds and test again.

5 Reserve some cooking water
Spoon out 2 ladlefuls of the pasta-cooking water. This starchy water can later be used to adjust the consistency of the pasta and sauce after they have been tossed together.

6 Drain the pasta
Put a colander in the sink and slowly pour the pasta away from you into the colander. Shake the colander to remove excess water; the pasta should still be slightly moist.

Cooking Fresh Filled Pasta

1 Salt the boiling water
Bring a large pot three-fourths full of water to a rolling boil. You'll need about 5 qt (5 l) of water to cook the pasta properly. Add about 2 tablespoons kosher salt to the water.

2 Add the pasta to the water
Drop 2 or 3 ravioli or tortellini into the pot at a time until you have added about half of them. It's best to cook fresh filled pasta in batches, so the pieces don't stick together.

3 Stir the pasta
Using a wooden spoon, gently stir the pasta occasionally to keep it from sticking. Adjust the heat so the water barely simmers. If the water boils too rapidly, the pasta may break open.

4 Watch for floating pasta
A reliable sign that ravioli or tortellini are finished cooking is when they begin to rise to the water's surface. This usually takes about 2 minutes.

5 Test the pasta for doneness
Scoop out 1 ravioli or tortellini with a slotted spoon. Using a paring knife, cut off a corner where the dough is doubled. Taste the corner; it should be tender but still slightly chewy.

6 Drain the pasta
Transfer the ravioli or tortellini a few at a time to a colander. After they have drained for a few seconds, pour them into a warmed serving bowl where they will be layered with sauce.

Cooking Dried Pasta

1 Salt the boiling water
Bring a large pot three-fourths full of water to a rolling boil. You'll need about 5 qt (5 l) of water to cook 1 lb (500 g) of pasta. Add about 2 tablespoons kosher salt to the water.

2 Add the pasta to the water
Add the dried pasta to the boiling water all at once. Use a wooden spoon to push any strands below the surface of the water if necessary, so all the strands cook evenly.

3 Stir the pasta
Using the spoon, gently stir the pasta from time to time to prevent it from sticking together. Adjust the heat if needed to keep the water at a boil, but don't let it boil over.

4 Test the pasta for doneness
After 7 minutes, remove a strand, let it cool slightly, and taste it. It should be tender but still slightly chewy, with a thin white line at the core. If not, cook for 1–2 minutes and test again.

5 Reserve some cooking water
Spoon out 2 ladlefuls of the pasta-cooking water. This starchy water can later be used to adjust the consistency of the pasta and sauce after they have been tossed together.

6 Drain the pasta
Place a colander in the sink and carefully pour the pasta away from you into the colander. Shake the colander just once; the pasta should still be slightly moist.

Cutting Herbs

1 Pick the leaves from the stems

Rinse and dry the herbs well. Using your fingers, pluck the leaves from the herb sprigs (in this case, parsley) and discard the stems. Gather the leaves into a pile on the cutting board.

Cutting Herbs into a Chiffonade

1 Pick the leaves from the stems

After rinsing the herb sprigs, dry them well (wet herbs will stick to the knife). Pick off the leaves, in this case basil, and discard any discolored or wilted leaves and the thick stems.

2 Stack the leaves

Stack 5 or 6 leaves on top of one another. It's best to choose leaves of a similar size. If you have some leaves that are slightly smaller, stack them on top.

2 Chop or mince the herbs

Rest your fingertips on the knife tip and rock the knife over the board to cut the leaves into coarse pieces (chopped) or fine pieces (minced). Stop occasionally to clean the knife.

3 Roll up the leaves

Roll the stack of leaves lengthwise into a cylinder. Try to roll the leaves as tightly as possible.

4 Cut the leaves into thin ribbons

Using a chef's knife, cut the leaves crosswise into thin ribbons. These ribbons are known as a *chiffonade*.

Cleaning Mushrooms

1 Trim the stem

Using a paring knife, trim a thin slice from the base of the stem of each mushroom and discard. These pieces can be dry. If the stems are very tough, remove them completely.

2 Brush away the dirt

Using a mushroom brush, gently remove any dirt from the mushrooms. You can use a damp cloth or paper towel to wipe away any stubborn dirt.

Peeling Plum Tomatoes

1 Score the tomatoes

Use a paring knife to cut a small, shallow X in the blossom end, or bottom, of each plum (Roma) tomato. This process, known as *scoring*, will help you remove the skin quickly later.

2 Blanch the tomatoes

Bring a pot of water to a boil. Using a slotted spoon, plunge the tomatoes in the boiling water for 15–30 seconds, or until the skins are just loosened. This brief cooking is called *blanching*.

3 Shock the tomatoes

Use the slotted spoon to transfer the blanched tomatoes to a bowl of ice water. This process is known as *shocking*, and it will stop the tomatoes from cooking too much.

4 Peel off the tomato skins

As soon as the tomatoes are cool, remove them from the ice water. Use a paring knife to pull off the skin, starting at the X. The skin should now peel off quickly and easily.

Seeding & Dicing Plum Tomatoes

TECHNIQUE

1 Cut the tomato in half

Plum (Roma) tomatoes are a good choice for using in pasta dishes, as they have a high flesh-to-seed ratio. Use a chef's knife to cut peeled tomatoes in half lengthwise.

2 Squeeze and scoop out the seeds

Gently squeeze each tomato half over a bowl. Use a fingertip, if needed, to help scoop out the seed sacs and watery pulp.

TROUBLESHOOTING

After removing the seeds, you may see white or yellow patches that were not evident when the tomato was whole. These spots indicate poor flavor and texture; trim them away or discard the tomato.

3 Remove the stem

Use a paring knife to make a V-shaped cut in the top of each tomato half to remove the green stem. Take care not to remove too much of the tomato flesh when you cut.

4 Cut lengthwise slices

Place one of the tomato halves cut side down. Using a chef's knife, make a series of lengthwise cuts, about ¼ inch (6 mm) apart.

5 Cut the strips into dice

Line up the strips and cut them crosswise into ¼-inch dice. Push the dice aside to keep them separate from your work area. Repeat steps 3–5 with the remaining tomatoes.

Dicing Carrots

1 Trim the carrots

Start with good-quality, unblemished carrots. Use a vegetable peeler to remove the rough skin. Switch to a chef's knife and trim off the leafy tops and rootlike ends.

2 Cut the carrots into lengths

Cut the carrots into even lengths no longer than about 3 inches (7.5 cm). Shorter pieces are simpler to handle, making cutting and then dicing easier.

3 Create a flat surface

Before cutting each length of carrot, cut a thin slice from one side to create a flat surface. Turn the carrot piece onto this flat side to keep it stable while you cut.

4 Cut the lengths into slices

Cut the carrot piece lengthwise into slices as thick as you want the final dice to be. (For example, if you are aiming for ¼-inch/6-mm dice, cut the carrot into ¼-inch slices.)

5 Cut the slices into sticks

Stack 2 or 3 carrot slices and turn them so they are lying on their wide sides. Cut them lengthwise into sticks that are as thick as the first slices.

6 Cut the sticks into dice

Cut the carrot sticks crosswise to create dice. Dicing carrots methodically creates evenly sized pieces that cook at the same rate. Repeat with the remaining carrot lengths.

Dicing Celery

1 Trim the root end
Start with firm, unblemished celery with fresh-looking leaves. Using a chef's knife, trim the head of the celery as needed where the stalks meet the root end. Rinse the stalks.

2 Chop the leaves (optional)
The leaves are used in some dishes to provide extra celery flavor. Cut the leaves from the stalks and chop as directed in a recipe, usually coarsely.

TROUBLESHOOTING
Some celery today is string free, but you may still encounter stringy stalks. The outside ribs may have a tough outer layer as well. To remove this layer or any strings, run a vegetable peeler over the stalk.

3 Cut the celery into lengths
Cut the celery stalks into even lengths no longer than about 3 inches (7.5 cm). Shorter pieces are simpler to handle, making slicing and then dicing easier.

4 Cut the lengths into sticks
Cut the celery pieces lengthwise into sticks as thick as you want the final dice to be. (For example, if you are aiming for ¼-inch/6-mm dice, cut the celery into ¼-inch-thick sticks.)

5 Cut the sticks into dice
Cut the celery sticks crosswise to create dice. Dicing celery methodically creates evenly sized pieces that cook at the same rate. Repeat with the remaining celery lengths.

Dicing an Onion

1 Cut the onion in half

Using a chef's knife, cut the onion in half lengthwise, through the root end. This makes it easier to peel and gives each half a flat side for stability when making your cuts.

2 Peel and trim the onion

Using a paring knife, pick up the edge of the onion's papery skin at the stem end and pull it away. You may also need to remove the first layer of onion if it, too, has rough or papery patches.

3 Place the onion on a board

Trim each end neatly, leaving some of the root intact to help hold the onion half together. Place an onion half, flat side down, on a cutting board with the root end facing away from you.

4 Cut the onion lengthwise

Hold the onion securely on either side. Using a chef's knife, make a series of lengthwise cuts as thick as you want the final dice to be. Do not cut all the way through the root end.

5 Cut the onion horizontally

Spread your fingers across the onion to help keep it together. Turn the knife blade parallel to the cutting board and make a series of horizontal cuts as thick as you want the final dice to be.

6 Cut the onion crosswise

Still holding the onion together with your fingers, cut it crosswise to make dice. Dicing an onion in this methodical way gives you pieces that cook evenly.

Working with Garlic

1 Loosen the garlic peel

Using the flat side of a chef's knife, firmly press against the clove. If you plan to mince the garlic, it's fine to smash it. If you are slicing it, use light pressure to keep the clove intact.

2 Peel and halve the clove

The pressure from the knife will cause the garlic peel to split. Grasp the peel with your fingers, pull it away, and then discard it. Cut the clove in half lengthwise to create flat sides.

TROUBLESHOOTING

You may see a small green sprout running through the middle of the garlic clove, which, if left in, could impart a bitter flavor to the dish. Use the tip of a paring knife to pop out the sprout and discard it.

3 Cut the garlic into slices

Working with one clove half at a time, use the knife to cut the garlic into very thin slices. Use the slices, or, if chopping or mincing, gather the slices in a pile in the center of the cutting board.

4 Chop the garlic

Rest the fingertips of one hand on top of the tip of the knife. Move the heel of the knife in a rhythmic up-and-down motion over the garlic slices until coarsely chopped.

5 Mince the garlic

Stop occasionally to clean the knife of garlic bits and gather them in a compact pile on the board. Continue to chop until the garlic pieces are very fine, or *minced*.

3

Fresh Pasta

Making fresh pasta will become simpler with time, and soon you will look forward to both handling the satiny dough and tasting the tender results. First, you will practice rolling, cutting, shaping, and filling a variety of fresh pastas. Then, you will cook them to the perfect point of tenderness. Finally, you will toss or layer the pastas with a number of sauces that match their subtle qualities.

Fettuccine with Bolognese Sauce

Bolognese sauce owes its rich, deep flavor to long, slow cooking and to starting with a *soffrito*, the mixture of carrot, onion, celery, and pancetta that forms the base of the sauce. The finished sauce should be delicate and creamy (helped, in part, by the addition of milk) and cling nicely to the pasta strands when tossed.

1 Dice the pancetta

Stack the pancetta slices on a cutting board. Using a chef's knife, cut the stack into strips about ¼-inch (6 mm) wide. Then make a second series of cuts perpendicular to the first cuts, again spacing them about ¼-inch apart, to create ¼-inch dice. Put the diced pancetta in a bowl and set aside.

2 Dice the vegetables

If you are not sure how to dice carrots, celery, and onions, turn to pages 42, 43, and 44. First, dice the carrots: Peel the carrots with a vegetable peeler, then use a chef's knife to cut them into ¼-inch dice. Then, dice the celery: Use the knife to trim the ends of the celery stalk and dice it into the same-sized pieces as the carrots. Finally, dice the onion: Cut the onion in half lengthwise and peel each half. One at a time, place the onion halves, cut side down, on the cutting board. Alternately make a series of lengthwise cuts, parallel cuts, then crosswise cuts to create ¼-inch (6-mm) dice. Be sure to stop just short of the root end; this holds the onion together as you cut. Remember: It's more important that your vegetables are cut into uniform-sized pieces than that your vegetable cuts are perfect. The more you practice, the more skilled you will become at using a knife.

3 Cook the *soffrito*

Select a large, wide, heavy-bottomed nonreactive pan; I use a sauté pan about 10 inches (25 cm) wide and 4 inches (10 cm) deep. Place the pan over medium-low heat and add the butter. When the butter has melted and the foam begins to subside, add the carrots, celery, onion, and pancetta and spread the ingredients evenly over the bottom of the pan with a wooden spoon or spatula. Cook, stirring occasionally, until all the ingredients are very tender, about 30 minutes. When ready, they should be a rich golden brown and smell like caramel. If you think that the ingredients are beginning to brown too much, reduce the heat slightly and stir in a spoonful or two of warm water to slow the cooking.

4 Brown the meats

Add the ground pork and ground beef to the pan and stir well. Raise the heat to medium and cook, stirring often to break up the meat lumps, until the meats are lightly browned, crumbly, and their juices have evaporated, which will take about 20 minutes. Try not to let the meats become crisp or dark brown, or they will not absorb the other flavors in the sauce and the desired creaminess of the finished dish will be affected.

For the Bolognese sauce

2 oz (60 g) thick-cut pancetta

2 small carrots

1 stalk celery

1 yellow onion

2 tablespoons unsalted butter

½ lb (250 g) ground (minced) pork

½ lb (250 g) ground (minced) beef chuck

½ cup (4 fl oz/125 ml) dry red wine such as Barbera

1 cup (6 oz/185 g) drained and chopped canned Italian peeled tomatoes

1–2 tablespoons tomato paste

2 cups (16 fl oz/500 ml) canned low-sodium beef broth, plus a little extra, if needed, to keep the sauce moist

1 cup (8 fl oz/250 ml) whole milk

1 teaspoon kosher salt

¼ teaspoon freshly ground pepper

¼ teaspoon freshly grated nutmeg

For the fresh egg pasta dough

2½ cups (12½ oz/390 g) unbleached all-purpose (plain) flour, plus extra for dusting

4 large eggs

2 teaspoons extra-virgin olive oil

Kosher salt for cooking the pasta

2 oz (60 g) Parmigiano-Reggiano cheese, freshly grated, for serving, if desired

MAKES 4 MAIN-COURSE SERVINGS OR 6–8 FIRST-COURSE SERVINGS

*Deglazing the browned
vegetables and meats
with wine adds complexity
and depth to this
long-simmered sauce.*

Using a food processor and pasta machine makes quick work of mixing, kneading, and rolling out fresh pasta dough.

5 Simmer the sauce

Add the wine to the pan, scraping the bottom to dislodge any browned bits. Cook until the wine evaporates, about 2 minutes. Stir in the tomatoes, 1 tablespoon of the tomato paste, the broth, milk, salt, pepper, and nutmeg. Heat the mixture until small bubbles begin to form on the surface, then reduce the heat to very low and continue to cook, stirring occasionally, for about 1 hour. (If, during cooking, the sauce seems too thick or threatens to scorch, add a little more broth.) Partially cover the pan and continue cooking the sauce on the lowest heat setting until it is thick and dark brown, 1–1½ hours longer. If you prefer a deeper red color and more tomato flavor, add 1 tablespoon more tomato paste after the first hour of cooking. As the sauce cooks, mash the meat and vegetables with the back of the spoon to break up any large pieces; this will help make the sauce smoother. When the sauce is ready, use a large spoon to skim off and discard any grease that floats on the surface. Cover the pan and set aside.

6 Mix the pasta dough and lightly knead it by hand

If you need help making fresh egg pasta dough, turn to page 22. Put 2 cups (10 oz/315 g) of the flour in a food processor fitted with the metal blade. Set the remaining ½ cup (2½ oz/75 g) flour nearby. Add the eggs and olive oil and process until the flour is evenly moistened and crumbly, about 10 seconds. Continue to process, adding the reserved flour 1 tablespoon at a time if needed, for about 30 seconds. A loose ball of dough will form on top of the blade. Dust a rough work surface and your hands with flour and put the ball of dough in the center. Knead the dough until it feels damp but not sticky and is an even yellow color. This will take only a minute or two. Shape the dough into a ball, cover it with a large overturned bowl, and let it rest for 30 minutes.

7 Knead the dough with a pasta machine

For help with kneading and rolling out fresh pasta dough, turn to page 32. Cut the dough into 4 equal pieces. Slip 3 of the pieces back under the bowl and flatten 1 piece into a disk about ½ inch (12 mm) thick. Turn the dial on the pasta machine to the widest setting and dust the rollers with flour. Crank the disk through the rollers. Fold the dough into thirds, dust 1 side with flour, and roll it through again. Repeat 8–10 times until the dough is smooth and satiny.

8 Roll out the dough into a sheet

Continue passing the dough through the rollers, moving the dial 1 notch narrower after each pass and lightly flouring the dough if it seems sticky (you don't need to fold it at this stage), until it is about 1/16 inch (2 mm) thick, usually after rolling on the second-to-last setting.

9 Let the pasta dry slightly

Cut the pasta sheet into sections about 10 inches (25 cm) long. Lay the sections flat on a lightly floured rimmed baking sheet, layering them as needed and separating the layers with floured lint-free kitchen towels. Repeat steps 7–9 with the remaining dough pieces. Let dry for 10–20 minutes.

10 Cut the pasta into fettuccine

For more details on cutting fresh fettuccine, turn to page 33. Secure the fettuccine-cutting attachment (for the widest strands) onto the pasta machine and attach the crank. One at a time, insert a section of dough into the blades and turn the crank to pass it through, creating strands about ¼ inch (6 mm) wide. Spread them out on a lightly floured rimmed baking sheet and let dry for 10–20 minutes while the water comes to a boil.

11 Cook the fettuccine

Preheat the oven to 200°F (95°C) and place individual shallow bowls in the oven to warm. To find out more about cooking fresh fettuccine, turn to page 36. Bring a large pot three-fourths full of water to a rolling boil and add about 2 tablespoons salt. Add the pasta all at once and stir it gently to prevent sticking. Let the pasta cook, stirring occasionally, until it is tender but still slightly chewy (al dente) when you bite into a piece. This should take only 1½–2 minutes.

12 Adjust the seasonings in the sauce

While the pasta is cooking, reheat the sauce over medium-low heat. Taste the warmed sauce and evaluate the seasonings. If the sauce tastes dull, add a bit more salt. If you think it needs more spice, add more pepper or nutmeg. Mix each seasoning in a little at a time until you achieve a flavor that you like. Keep in mind that the flavor will be diluted once it is mixed with the pasta.

13 Drain the fettuccine

Transfer 2 ladlefuls of pasta-cooking water to a heatproof container; you'll use it to adjust the consistency of the dish when you toss it. Pour the pasta into a colander to drain, then shake the colander to remove the excess water. Don't let the strands get too dry, or they will stick together.

14 Toss the fettuccine with the sauce

Add the drained pasta to the pan with the sauce. Using 2 wooden spoons or spatulas, toss the ingredients together; bring the pasta from the bottom of the pan to the top until it is evenly coated with the sauce. To do this thoroughly, plan on about 30 seconds of tossing. If the mixture looks dry as you toss, drizzle a little of the reserved pasta-cooking water over the pasta and continue to toss. Every strand of pasta should be evenly coated with the sauce.

15 Serve the dish

Using a pasta fork, divide the sauced pasta evenly among the warmed bowls, using a silicone spatula to scrape out any remaining sauce from the pan. Serve right away, passing the cheese at the table, if desired.

Serving ideas

On traditional Italian-restaurant menus, pasta dishes are listed as a separate course, meant to be eaten before the meat, poultry, or fish course. In the United States, these same dishes are often convenient one-dish meals. The beauty of pasta is that it lends itself to serving in a variety of ways: a first course for a formal dinner, heaped on a platter for a casual gathering, or in individual bowls for a hearty weeknight meal.

First-course serving (top left)
When serving pasta as a first course, try twirling the sauced pasta on a large fork to make a pretty presentation for your guests.

Family-style platter (left)
For a casual meal, pile the sauced pasta on a large warmed platter and pass it family style at the dinner table. Remember to include the serving utensils so that diners can help themselves.

Individual serving (above)
Serve strand pastas such as this one in warmed shallow bowls. A diner can push his or her fork against the side of the bowl and twirl the strands against it to help the pasta stay on the fork.

Fettuccine Alfredo

Tender, porous, fresh fettuccine is the perfect pasta to absorb a thick, creamy sauce built from just a trio of ingredients: butter, cream, and Parmigiano-Reggiano cheese. When tossed, the pasta ribbons should be lightly, yet fully coated with the sauce, whose richness is tempered by the salty, mellow cheese.

1 Mix the pasta dough

If you need help making fresh egg pasta dough, turn to page 22. Put 2 cups (10 oz/315 g) of the flour in a food processor fitted with the metal blade. Set the remaining ½ cup (2½ oz/75 g) flour nearby. Add the eggs and olive oil and process until the flour is evenly moistened and crumbly, about 10 seconds. Continue to process, adding the reserved flour 1 tablespoon at a time if needed, for about 30 seconds. A loose ball of dough will form on top of the blade.

2 Lightly knead the dough by hand

Dust a rough work surface a[nd] dough in the center of the work s[urface] away from you, then lift and rota[te] the dough with flour if necessary [...] yellow with no streaks of flour. Th[en] into a ball, cover it with a large o[...]

3 Knead the dough with a [...]

For help with kneading and [...] Secure the pasta machine onto y[our] flour a rimmed baking sheet and [...] knife, cut the dough into 4 equa[l ...] bowl to keep the surface from dry[ing ...] ½ inch (12 mm) thick. Turn the [...] and dust the rollers with flour. Cr[ank ...] into thirds, dust 1 side with flour, and roll it through again. Repeat 8–10 times until the dough is smooth and satiny.

4 Roll out the dough into a sheet

Continue passing the dough through the rollers, moving the dial 1 notch narrower after each pass and lightly flouring the dough if it seems sticky (you don't need to fold it at this stage). When it's ready, the dough should be about 1/16 inch (2 mm) thick, usually after rolling on the second-to-last setting, and you should be able to see the silhouette of your hand through the dough when you hold it up to the light.

For the fresh egg pasta dough

2½ cups (12½ oz/390 g) unbleached all-purpose (plain) flour, plus extra for dusting

4 large eggs

2 teaspoons extra-virgin olive oil

For the Alfredo sauce

3 oz (90 g) Parmigiano-Reggiano cheese

4 tablespoons (2 oz/60 g) unsalted butter

1 cup (8 fl oz/250 ml) heavy (double) cream

½ teaspoon kosher salt

Kosher salt for cooking the pasta

Freshly ground pepper, optional

MAKES 6 MAIN-COURSE SERVINGS OR 8 FIRST-COURSE SERVINGS

CHEF'S TIP

To distinguish true Parmesan cheese from the many impostors, look for the words "Parmigiano-Reggiano" stenciled on the rind.

[Handwritten note:]
For our typical 140g dose of pasta Fresca, use about a half recipe:
50g Parmigiano-Regiano
30g Butter &or Romano Pecorino
½ cup half & half
+ 2 tsp Flour
teaspoons!

5 Let the pasta dry slightly

Cut the pasta sheet into sections about 10 inches (25 cm) long. Lay the sections flat on the floured baking sheet, layering them as needed and separating the layers with floured lint-free kitchen towels. Repeat steps 3–5 with the remaining dough pieces. Let dry for 10–20 minutes. (The drying will firm up the dough and make it easier to cut.)

6 Cut the pasta into fettuccine

For more details on cutting fresh fettuccine, turn to page 33. Secure the fettuccine-cutting attachment (for the widest strands) onto the pasta machine and attach the crank. One at a time, insert a section of dough into the blades and turn the crank to pass it through, creating strands about ¼ inch (6 mm) wide. Spread them out on a lightly floured rimmed baking sheet and let dry for 10–20 minutes while you make the Alfredo sauce.

7 Make the sauce

Finely grate the cheese using the small grating holes of a box grater-shredder or a rasp grater. Set the cheese aside. Place a 12-inch (30-cm) frying pan over medium-low heat and add the butter. When the butter has melted, add the cream and salt and heat until small bubbles start to form, then let it simmer until it is slightly thickened, about 5 minutes. (This thickening step is critical; if the sauce is too thin, it will sit in a pool beneath the pasta, rather than nicely coat the strands.) Remove the pan from the heat. While the sauce is simmering, preheat the oven to 200°F (95°C) and place individual shallow bowls in the oven to warm.

8 Cook the fettuccine

To find out more about cooking fresh fettuccine, turn to page 36. Bring a large pot three-fourths full of water to a rolling boil and add about 2 tablespoons salt. Add the pasta all at once and stir it gently to prevent sticking. Let the pasta cook, stirring occasionally, until it is tender but still slightly chewy (al dente) when you bite into a piece. This should take only 1½–2 minutes.

CHEF'S TIP

Two tablespoons of salt may seem like a lot to add to the cooking water, but don't worry. Italian cooks believe that for the best tasting pasta, the water should be as salty as the sea.

9 Adjust the seasonings in the sauce

While the pasta is cooking, reheat the sauce over low heat. Taste the warmed sauce and evaluate the seasonings. Keep in mind that the cheese that will be added contributes a good deal of salt. If you feel the sauce needs either salt or pepper (pepper is optional, as some people don't like the look of the black flecks in the white sauce), mix them in a little bit at a time and taste again until you are happy with the balance of flavors.

11 >>

CHEF'S TIP

To warm serving bowls quickly for pasta, ladle some of the hot pasta-cooking water into the bowls before draining the pasta. Carefully swirl the water in the bowls, pour it out, and then dry the bowls and add the sauced pasta.

10 Drain the fettuccine

Transfer 2 ladlefuls of pasta-cooking water to a heatproof container; you'll use it to adjust the consistency of the dish when you toss it. Pour the pasta into a colander to drain, then shake the colander to remove the excess water. Don't let the strands get too dry, or they will stick together.

11 Toss the fettuccine with the sauce

Add the drained pasta to the pan with the sauce, then add the Parmigiano-Reggiano cheese. Using 2 wooden spoons or spatulas, toss the ingredients together; bring the pasta from the bottom of the pan to the top until all the strands are evenly coated with the sauce and cheese. To do this thoroughly, plan on about 30 seconds of tossing.

12 Adjust the consistency of the dish

If the mixture looks dry as you toss, drizzle a little of the reserved pasta-cooking water over the pasta and continue to toss. Every strand of pasta should carry a light coating of sauce, giving the pasta a satiny, moist finish.

13 Serve the dish

Using a pasta fork, divide the sauced pasta evenly among the warmed bowls, using a silicone spatula to scrape out any remaining sauce from the pan. Serve right away.

Finishing touches

The rich, luxurious flavor of fettuccine Alfredo belies its simplicity. To enhance each serving further, try one of the following delicious ideas: A sprinkle of fresh nutmeg tempers the creaminess with a touch of spice. Shaved fresh white truffles or drizzles of truffle oil dress up the dish for a special occasion. Finally, shaved, instead of grated, Parmigiano-Reggiano cheese tops off the pasta with flair.

Nutmeg (top left)
Lightly dust each portion of pasta with freshly grated nutmeg. Don't go overboard; you'll need only about ⅛ teaspoon total for all 6 servings.

Truffle oil (left)
In autumn, shaved fresh white truffles are a prized addition to fettuccine Alfredo. Expensive and hard to find in the United States, you can replace them with a drizzle of white truffle oil.

Parmesan cheese shavings (above)
Instead of passing grated cheese at the table, offer a vegetable peeler and a wedge of Parmigiano-Reggiano to create thin shavings, which provide a visual and textural counterpoint.

Pasta with Cream Sauce Variations

Ribbons of fresh egg pasta such as fettuccine are traditionally paired with sauces based on butter and cream that nicely coat each strand yet won't overpower the mild flavor of the pasta itself. Once you have mastered the traditional Alfredo Sauce on page 55, turn to these variations to create additional fettuccine dishes dressed with rich, creamy sauces. Each of the six variations below features a carefully selected roster of ingredients, from spring vegetables to autumnal mushrooms to sweet butter and sage. All of the sauces cling beautifully to fresh, tender fettuccine. Each variation makes 6 main-course servings or 8 first-course servings.

Fettuccine Primavera

In *la primavera*—"the spring"—a quintet of sautéed vegetables can add freshness to the basic Alfredo sauce.

Make, roll, and cut Fresh Egg Pasta Dough (page 22) into fettuccine, then spread on a lightly floured baking sheet to dry.

Meanwhile, make the sauce: In a 12-inch (30-cm) frying pan over medium heat, melt 4 tablespoons (2 oz/60g) unsalted butter. Add 1 finely diced small yellow onion, 2 peeled and finely diced carrots, ¼ lb (125 g) green beans cut into ½-inch (12-mm) pieces, 1 cup (5 oz/155 g) asparagus tips (¾ inch/2 cm long), and ½ cup (2½ oz/75 g) diced red bell pepper (capsicum). Sauté the vegetables until slightly softened, about 5 minutes. Reduce the heat to medium-low, add 1 cup (8 fl oz/250 ml) heavy (double) cream, and simmer until thickened, about 5 minutes. Adjust the seasonings.

Cook the fettuccine for 1½–2 minutes, reserve some of the cooking water, and drain the pasta. Toss the fettuccine with the sauce and 3 oz (90 g) freshly grated Parmigiano-Reggiano cheese until evenly coated, adjusting the consistency with the cooking water. Serve right away.

Fettuccine with Peas, Peppers & Prosciutto

A quartet of complementary flavors makes a more substantial pasta dish.

Make, roll, and cut Fresh Egg Pasta Dough (page 22) into fettuccine, then spread on a lightly floured baking sheet to dry.

Meanwhile, cook the peas: Add 1 cup (5 oz/155 g) shelled English peas or frozen petite peas to boiling salted water and cook until tender, about 1 minute for fresh or 4 minutes for frozen. Drain the peas, immerse in cold water to halt the cooking, and drain again.

Make the sauce: In a 12-inch (30-cm) frying pan over medium-low heat, melt 4 tablespoons (2 oz/60g) unsalted butter. Add 1 cup (8 fl oz/250 ml) heavy (double) cream and simmer until thickened, about 5 minutes. Add 2 oz (60 g) diced prosciutto, 1 cup (6 oz/185 g) diced purchased roasted red bell peppers (capsicums), and the peas. Adjust the seasonings.

Cook the fettuccine for 1½–2 minutes, reserve some of the cooking water, and drain the pasta. Toss the fettuccine with the sauce and 3 oz (90 g) freshly grated Parmigiano-Reggiano cheese until evenly coated, adjusting the consistency with the cooking water. Serve right away.

Fettuccine with Gorgonzola & Cream

The addition of Gorgonzola results in a deeper, sharper flavor and added richness. Seek out Gorgonzola labeled *dolce* for a milder flavor or *naturale* for a stronger sauce.

Make, roll, and cut Fresh Egg Pasta Dough (page 22) into fettuccine, then spread on a lightly floured baking sheet to dry.

Meanwhile, make the sauce: In a 12-inch (30-cm) frying pan over medium-low heat, melt 2 tablespoons unsalted butter. Add 1 cup (8 fl oz/250 ml) heavy (double) cream and simmer until thickened, about 5 minutes. Adjust the seasonings.

Cook the fettuccine for 1½–2 minutes, reserve some of the cooking water, and drain the pasta. Toss the fettuccine with the sauce, 5 oz (155 g) crumbled Gorgonzola, and 3 oz (90 g) freshly grated Parmigiano-Reggiano cheese until evenly coated, adjusting the consistency with the cooking water. Serve right away.

Fettuccine with Mushrooms & Cream

When the cool autumn months arrive, the earthy flavor of mushrooms mixes well with a creamy sauce.

Make, roll, and cut Fresh Egg Pasta Dough (page 22) into fettuccine, then spread on a lightly floured baking sheet to dry.

Meanwhile, make the sauce: In a 12-inch (30-cm) frying pan over medium heat, melt 2 tablespoons unsalted butter. Add 10 oz (315 g) sliced fresh white mushrooms, 1 teaspoon kosher salt, and ⅛ teaspoon freshly ground pepper. Sauté until the mushroom juices evaporate and the mushrooms are golden brown, about 10 minutes. Reduce the heat to medium-low, add 1 cup (8 fl oz/250 ml) heavy (double) cream, and simmer until thickened, about 5 minutes. Stir in 2 tablespoons chopped fresh flat-leaf (Italian) parsley. Adjust the seasonings.

Cook the fettuccine for 1½–2 minutes, reserve some of the cooking water, and drain the pasta. Toss the fettuccine with the sauce until evenly coated, adjusting the consistency with the cooking water. Serve right away.

CHEF'S TIP
Fresh fettuccine is just one choice for pairing with these cream sauces; you can use other fresh, wide strands, too. Two choices, both wider than fettuccine, are pappardelle (1¼ inches/3 cm) and tagliatelle (½ inch/12 mm). To make them, first roll out the pasta thinly by hand with a rolling pin, then roll up each sheet into a cylinder and cut the strands crosswise with a chef's knife.

Fettuccine with Shrimp, Tomato & Cream

Sweet shrimp and tart tomatoes blend well with a delicate, creamy pasta sauce.

Make, roll, and cut Fresh Egg Pasta Dough (page 22) into fettuccine, then spread on a lightly floured baking sheet to dry.

In a 12-inch (30-cm) nonreactive frying pan over medium heat, melt 2 tablespoons unsalted butter. Add 1 finely diced shallot and sauté until softened, about 4 minutes. Add 10 oz (315 g) peeled, deveined, and chopped shrimp (prawns); 1 peeled, seeded, and diced plum (Roma) tomato; 1 teaspoon kosher salt; and ¼ teaspoon freshly ground pepper and sauté until the shrimp are opaque, 2–3 minutes. Reduce the heat to medium-low, add 1 cup (8 fl oz/250 ml) heavy (double) cream, and simmer until thickened, about 5 minutes. Stir in ¼ cup (⅓ oz/10 g) chopped fresh basil. Adjust the seasonings.

Cook the fettuccine for 1½–2 minutes, reserve some of the cooking water, and drain the pasta. Toss the fettuccine with the sauce until evenly coated, adjusting the consistency with the cooking water. Serve right away.

Spiced Fettuccine with Butter & Sage Sauce

Although there is no cream, this recipe bears a rich relation to Alfredo sauce because of its generous use of butter and cheese. It is accented by two distinctive flavors: aromatic sage in the sauce and black pepper in the pasta dough.

Make Fresh Egg Pasta Dough (page 22), mixing 1 teaspoon freshly ground pepper into the flour before adding the eggs. Roll and cut the dough into fettuccine, then spread on a lightly floured baking sheet to dry.

Meanwhile, make the sauce: In a 12-inch (30-cm) nonreactive frying pan over medium-low heat, combine ½ cup (4 oz/ 125 g) unsalted butter, ¼ cup (2 fl oz/ 60 ml) water, 3 or 4 fresh sage leaves, and ½ teaspoon kosher salt. Cook, stirring with a wooden spoon, just until the butter is melted. Remove from the heat. Adjust the seasonings.

Cook the fettuccine for 1½–2 minutes, reserve some of the cooking water, and drain the pasta. Toss the fettuccine with the sauce and 3 oz (90 g) freshly grated Parmigiano-Reggiano cheese until evenly coated, adjusting the consistency with the cooking water. Serve right away.

Orecchiette with Broccoli Rabe & Sausage

Broccoli rabe has a pleasantly bitter flavor that is an appealing contrast to the sweet pork sausages in this sauce. As you toss, both ingredients get trapped in the hollows of the little ear-shaped pasta, making every bite wonderfully flavorful. Prepare this dish in the cool-weather months, when broccoli rabe is in season.

1 Mix the pasta dough

If you need help making semolina pasta dough, turn to page 26. In a food processor fitted with the metal blade, combine the all-purpose and semolina flours and the salt. Pulse the machine a few times to mix the ingredients. With the processor running, pour ½ cup (4 fl oz/125 ml) of the warm water through the feed tube in a thin, steady stream, adding the remaining water 1 tablespoon at a time as needed to moisten the dough. After about 30 seconds, the dough should come together and form a loose ball on top of the blade. Remove the top of the processor and pinch the dough to check its texture; it should feel moist, but not sticky. If the dough seems too dry, add a teaspoon of water and process until blended. Do not add more water than is necessary, or the dough will be too soft to shape.

2 Knead the dough and let it rest

Dust a rough work surface and your hands with all-purpose flour and put the ball of dough in the center of the work surface. With the heel of one hand, push the ball of dough away from you. Lift it from the far side with your fingers, fold it back toward you, and then rotate the dough a quarter turn. Repeat the motion, dusting the dough with flour if necessary, until it feels damp but not sticky. This will take only a minute or two. Shape the dough into a ball, cover with a large overturned bowl, and let it rest for 30 minutes.

3 Divide the dough

If you are not sure how to shape orecchiette, turn to page 34. Clean the work surface, then dust it again with flour. Using a bench scraper or chef's knife, cut the ball of dough into 4 equal pieces, then shape the pieces into short cylinders. Place a cylinder of dough in the center of the work surface. Using the fingers of both hands, roll the dough back and forth over the surface, gradually shifting your hands to the ends, to elongate it slowly into a narrow log. Stop rolling when the log is about ½ inch (12 mm) in diameter. Repeat with the remaining dough cylinders. Using the bench scraper or knife, cut the logs into ½-inch pieces.

4 Shape the orecchiette

Grasp the handle of a table knife, extending your index finger along one side of the blade. Using the tip of the knife, flatten each piece of dough and drag it slightly over the work surface to form a disk. Push each disk over the tip of your thumb to form a small cup. Put the finished orecchiette, separated so they don't stick together, on a lightly floured rimmed baking sheet and set aside to dry slightly. ➤

For the semolina pasta dough

2 cups (10 oz/315 g) unbleached all-purpose (plain) flour, plus extra for dusting

¾ cup (4 oz/125 g) finely ground semolina flour (do not substitute coarsely ground)

1 teaspoon kosher salt

¾ cup (6 fl oz/180 ml) warm water (105°F/40°C), or as needed

For the broccoli rabe and sausage sauce

2 large bunches broccoli rabe, about 2 lb (1 kg) total weight

½ lb (250 g) Italian sweet pork sausages

4 tablespoons (2 fl oz/60 ml) olive oil

4 large cloves garlic, thinly sliced (page 45)

¼ teaspoon red pepper flakes

1 teaspoon kosher salt

¼ cup (2 fl oz/60 ml) water

Kosher salt for cooking the pasta

2 oz (60 g) *pecorino romano* or Parmigiano-Reggiano cheese, freshly grated

MAKES 4–6 SERVINGS

CHEF'S TIP
The need to rinse pasta after cooking is an old wives' tale. Doing so removes some of the starch that helps the sauce adhere to the pasta.

5 Prepare the broccoli rabe
Trim any wilted or yellow leaves from the broccoli rabe and cut off the tough stem ends, usually 1–2 inches (2.5–5 cm). Stack the broccoli rabe on a cutting board and use a chef's knife to cut it crosswise into strips ½ inch (12 mm) wide.

6 Brown the sausages
Use a paring knife to make a small slit down the length of the sausages, then pull off and discard the casings. Place a 12-inch (30-cm) frying pan over medium-high heat and add 1 tablespoon of the olive oil. When the oil appears to shimmer, add the sausage meat and cook, breaking up the meat with a wooden spoon, until it is nicely browned, about 15 minutes. Using a slotted spoon, transfer the sausage to a cutting board and, if necessary, chop the meat into pieces the size of peas.

7 Make the sauce
Return the pan to medium heat and add the remaining 3 tablespoons oil. When the oil appears to shimmer, add the garlic and red pepper flakes and cook, stirring frequently, until the garlic is lightly golden, about 2 minutes. Add the broccoli rabe and salt, cover the pan, and cook for 5 minutes; the broccoli rabe will dramatically reduce in volume. Stir in the browned sausage and the water and cook, stirring, until the water evaporates and the broccoli rabe is tender (bite into a piece to check it), about 5 minutes longer. Remove the pan from the heat.

8 Adjust the seasonings
Taste the sauce. If you feel it tastes dull, stir in a bit more salt or red pepper flakes until the flavor is to your liking. Note that the flavor will mellow somewhat when mixed with the pasta.

9 Cook and drain the orecchiette
Preheat the oven to 200°F (95°C) and place individual bowls in the oven to warm. Bring a large pot three-fourths full of water to a rolling boil and add about 2 tablespoons salt. Add the pasta all at once and stir it gently to prevent sticking. Let the pasta cook, stirring occasionally, until it is tender but still slightly chewy (al dente) when you bite into a piece, 3–5 minutes. While the pasta is cooking, reheat the sauce over medium heat. Transfer 2 ladlefuls of pasta-cooking water to a heatproof container. Pour the pasta into a colander to drain, then shake the colander to remove the excess water. Don't let the orecchiette get too dry, or they will stick together.

10 Toss the orecchiette with the sauce
Add the drained pasta to the pan with the sauce and, using 2 wooden spoons or spatulas, toss the pasta until it is evenly coated with the sauce. If the mixture looks dry, add a little of the pasta-cooking water and continue to toss until the dish looks moist. Remove from the heat, add the cheese, and toss again.

11 Serve the dish
Divide the sauced pasta evenly among the warmed bowls, using a silicone spatula to scrape out any remaining sauce from the pan. Serve right away.

Shaped Pasta Variations

Semolina pasta dough, which is made with hard-wheat flour and no eggs, is stiff and pliable so that you can easily shape it into ear-shaped orecchiette. The same flour-and-water dough can be formed into small football-shaped pasta called *cavatelli*, which can be used interchangeably in recipes calling for orecchiette. Chunky or thick sauces are ideal with both shapes, as their ingredients are captured inside the crevices of the pasta. Once you learn how to make Orecchiette with Broccoli Rabe & Sausage (page 63), you can easily make the following recipes by substituting a few ingredients or using a different sauce. Each variation makes 4 to 6 servings.

Orecchiette with Fresh Tomatoes & Mozzarella

In summer I like to use a traditional trio of fresh tomatoes and basil (both at their seasonal peaks) along with fresh mozzarella to make an uncooked sauce. This sauce is perfect with my homemade orecchiette.

Make Fresh Semolina Pasta Dough (page 26) and shape it into orecchiette (page 34). Spread the pasta shapes on a lightly floured baking sheet to dry slightly.

Meanwhile, put 3 peeled, seeded, and diced plum (Roma) tomatoes in a warmed large serving bowl. Add 1 minced garlic clove and 20 fresh basil leaves, cut into a chiffonade. Stir in ¼ cup (2 fl oz/60 ml) extra-virgin olive oil, 1 teaspoon kosher salt, and ⅛ teaspoon freshly ground pepper. Add ½ lb (250 g) diced fresh mozzarella cheese and stir well. Adjust the seasonings.

Cook the orecchiette for 3–5 minutes, reserve some of the cooking water, and drain the pasta. Toss the orecchiette with the tomato mixture until evenly coated, adjusting the consistency with the cooking water. The mozzarella will soften and begin to melt, forming a creamy sauce. Serve right away.

Cavatelli with Arrabbiata Sauce & Cauliflower

In Italy, cauliflower is often paired with chile-flecked *arrabbiata* sauce. I like to match these ingredients with *cavatelli*.

Make Fresh Semolina Pasta Dough (page 26) and shape it into *cavatelli* (page 35). Spread the pasta shapes on a lightly floured baking sheet to dry slightly.

Meanwhile, make 1 batch Arrabbiata Sauce (page 95). Add 3 cups (6 oz/185 g) cauliflower pieces (¾-inch/2-cm pieces) and ¼ cup (2 fl oz/60 ml) water to the sauce, cover the pan, and cook until the cauliflower is softened, about 15 minutes longer. Keep the sauce warm.

Cook the *cavatelli* for 3–5 minutes, reserve some of the cooking water, and drain the pasta. Transfer the *cavatelli* to the pan with the sauce. Toss the pasta with the sauce until it is well coated and the cauliflower is evenly distributed, adjusting the consistency with the cooking water. Serve right away.

Cavatelli with Marinara Sauce & Arugula

Here, marinara sauce provides the same depth of flavor as sausage, while peppery arugula stands in for bitter broccoli rabe for a vegetarian version of my original recipe.

Make Fresh Semolina Pasta Dough (page 26) and shape it into *cavatelli* (page 35). Spread the pasta shapes on a lightly floured baking sheet to dry slightly.

Meanwhile, make 1 batch Marinara Sauce (page 94) and keep it warm.

Cook the *cavatelli* for 3–5 minutes, reserve some of the cooking water, and drain the pasta. Transfer the *cavatelli* to the pan with the sauce. Tear 2 cups (2 oz/60 g) arugula (rocket) leaves into bite-sized pieces and add them to the pan. Toss the pasta with the sauce until it is well coated and the arugula is evenly distributed, adjusting the consistency with the cooking water. Sprinkle with ½ cup (2 oz/60 g) freshly grated Parmigiano-Reggiano cheese and toss again to mix. Serve right away.

Ravioli

The best ravioli are light and delicate and conceal a distinctive filling. Here, beef sirloin seasoned with vegetables, Parmigiano-Reggiano cheese, and red wine is tucked inside squares of tender fresh pasta. A quickly made, deep-red tomato sauce provides a colorful and flavorful contrast to the plump, ivory squares.

1 Prepare the ingredients for the filling

If you are not sure how to dice the carrot, celery, and onion, turn to pages 42, 43, and 44. First, dice the carrot: Peel the carrot with a vegetable peeler, then use a chef's knife to cut it into ¼-inch (6-mm) dice. Then, dice the celery: Use the knife to trim the ends of the celery stalk and dice it into the same-sized pieces as the carrot. Finally, dice the onion: Cut the onion in half lengthwise and peel each half. One at a time, place the onion halves, cut side down, on the cutting board. Alternately make a series of lengthwise cuts, parallel cuts, then crosswise cuts to create ¼-inch (6-mm) dice. Stop just short of the root end; this holds the onion together as you cut. After dicing the vegetables, finely grate the cheese using the small grating holes of a box grater-shredder or a rasp grater. Measure out ½ cup (2 oz/60 g) packed grated cheese for the filling and set the remaining cheese aside.

2 Cook the vegetables and beef

Place a large frying pan over medium heat and add the butter. When the butter has melted and the foam begins to subside, add the carrot, celery, and onion. Cook, stirring occasionally with a wooden spoon, until the vegetables are golden and tender, about 15 minutes. Add the ground beef, salt, and pepper and break up the meat into small pieces with the spoon. Stir well and cook until the meat is no longer red and its juices have evaporated, about 10 minutes. Add the wine, bring to a simmer, and cook until the wine evaporates, about 2 minutes. Remove the pan from the heat and let the filling cool slightly.

3 Process the filling

Scrape the filling mixture into a food processor fitted with the metal blade and pulse until finely chopped. Add the eggs and the ½ cup cheese and pulse just until blended. Add the bread crumbs and pulse to blend. Scrape the filling into a bowl. Cover and chill the filling for at least 1 hour or up to overnight. This will help marry the flavors and firm up the filling so it is easier to work with.

4 Adjust the seasonings

To check the seasonings, it's a good idea to fry a small nugget of the filling mixture to get a better sense of how it will taste when it's fully cooked. Heat the olive oil in a small frying pan over medium heat until it appears to shimmer. Place a small spoonful of the filling in the pan and cook until browned on both sides, about 3 minutes. Using tongs, remove the nugget from the pan and transfer to a plate. When the nugget has cooled slightly, taste it and evaluate the seasonings. If you feel it tastes a little bland, mix a small amount of salt or pepper into the remaining filling mixture.

For the beef filling

1 carrot

1 large stalk celery

1 small yellow onion

⅓ lb (155 g) Parmigiano-Reggiano cheese, plus a little extra for serving, if desired

2 tablespoons unsalted butter

¾ lb (375 g) ground (minced) beef sirloin

¾ teaspoon kosher salt

⅛ teaspoon freshly ground pepper

½ cup (4 fl oz/125 ml) dry red wine such as Barbera

2 large eggs

¼ cup (1 oz/30 g) plain fine dried bread crumbs

1 tablespoon olive oil for frying the filling "nugget"

1 batch Fresh Egg Pasta Dough (page 22)

Kosher salt for cooking the pasta

1 batch Classic Tomato Sauce (page 92)

MAKES ABOUT 60 RAVIOLI, OR 6–8 SERVINGS

CHEF'S TIP

Always read the recipe ingredients list before you begin to assemble your mise en place (page 17). For this recipe, note that you will need to have the pasta dough and sauce already made before you begin.

A fluted pastry wheel will crimp and seal the edges of the ravioli at the same time. It makes a uniform pattern that gives the ravioli a finished look.

When making ravioli, use the pasta sheets as soon as possible after rolling them out. If the sheets dry too long, the pasta will be difficult to seal.

5 Knead the dough with a pasta machine

For help with kneading and rolling out fresh pasta dough, turn to page 32. Secure the pasta machine onto your work surface and attach the crank. Cut the dough into 4 equal pieces, then slip 3 of the pieces back under the bowl. Flatten 1 dough piece into a disk about ½ inch (12 mm) thick. Turn the dial on the pasta machine to the widest setting and dust the rollers with flour. Crank the disk through the rollers. Fold the dough into thirds, dust 1 side with flour, and roll it through again. Repeat 8–10 times until the dough is smooth and satiny.

6 Roll out the dough into a sheet

Continue passing the dough through the rollers, moving the dial 1 notch narrower after each pass and lightly flouring the dough if it seems sticky (you don't need to fold it at this stage). When it's ready, the dough should be about 1/16 inch (2 mm) thick, usually after rolling on the second-to-last setting.

7 Cut the sheet into sections

Cut the pasta sheet into sections about 17 inches (43 cm) long and 4 inches (10 cm) wide. Lay the sections flat on a lightly floured rimmed baking sheet, layering them as needed and separating the layers with floured lint-free kitchen towels. Repeat steps 5–7 with the remaining dough pieces. The pasta sections should not be dried before using.

8 Fill the ravioli

Lay 1 section of pasta on a floured work surface. Fold it in half lengthwise to mark the center, then unfold it. Beginning about 1 inch (2.5 cm) from one of the short ends, place teaspoonfuls of the filling about 1 inch apart in a straight row down the center of one side of the fold. Don't be tempted to add more filling; overstuffing can cause the ravioli to burst during cooking. Dip a pastry brush in cool water and lightly brush around the filling; this acts as a glue that keeps the filling tightly sealed inside the pasta. Fold the dough over the filling.

9 Seal and separate the ravioli

Using your fingers, mold the dough around the filling to eliminate any air pockets (these could also cause the ravioli to burst) and press the layers together firmly. Using a fluted pastry wheel, cut along the length on both sides and across the top and bottom of the filled strip, crimping the edges and trimming away about ⅛ inch (3 mm), then cut between the mounds, making small pillow-shaped ravioli and sealing all the edges. Place the ravioli in a single layer on 2 or 3 lightly floured rimmed baking sheets. Do not let them touch or they will stick together. Fill, seal, and separate the remaining dough sections in the same way.

10 **Ready your ingredients and equipment for cooking**
Since filled pasta takes only a short time to cook and should be served right away, it's a good idea to have everything you need close at hand before cooking it. Preheat the oven to 200°F (95°C) and place a large, shallow serving bowl and individual plates in the oven to warm. Bring a large pot three-fourths full of water to a rolling boil and add about 2 tablespoons salt. While the water is heating, put the tomato sauce in a saucepan and bring it to a simmer over medium-low heat. Have ready a colander set over a bowl or in the sink.

11 **Cook the ravioli**
To find out more about cooking fresh filled pasta, turn to page 37. A few at a time, drop half of the ravioli into the boiling water. (Cooking the ravioli in batches prevents them from sticking together and falling apart.) Reduce the heat slightly so that the water barely simmers; if the water boils too rapidly, it could cause the ravioli to break open. Stir the ravioli gently with a slotted spoon and cook until they rise to the surface. This should take only about 2 minutes. To test the ravioli for doneness, use the slotted spoon to remove 1 ravioli and use a paring knife to cut off one of the corners. Bite into it; the pasta should be tender but still slightly chewy (al dente).

12 **Drain and sauce the ravioli**
Gently layering, rather than tossing, the ravioli with the sauce helps to keep them from splitting open. Pour about one-third of the hot sauce into the warmed serving bowl. With the slotted spoon, scoop out the ravioli and place them in the colander to drain for a few seconds. Transfer the drained ravioli to the bowl with the sauce. Spoon on another one-third of the sauce and half of the remaining grated cheese. Cover the bowl with foil to keep the ingredients warm while you cook the remaining ravioli. Turn up the heat so the water returns to a rolling boil. Add the remaining ravioli, reduce the heat to a bare simmer, and cook them as you did the first half. Drain the second batch of ravioli in the same way, pour it on top of the first batch, and top with the remaining sauce and cheese.

13 **Serve the dish**
Using a large spoon, divide the ravioli and sauce among the warmed plates. Sprinkle with more cheese, if desired, and serve right away.

CHEF'S TIP
If your ravioli seem very fragile while you are making them, freeze them, right on their baking sheets, for up to 20 minutes. The firm, partially frozen ravioli will be easier to pick up and drop into the cooking water.

Serving ideas

The traditional shape for ravioli is square, but I sometimes like to make filled pasta pillows in other shapes, too. Circles and half-moons, the latter known as mezzelune *in Italy, are good examples. If you don't have a fluted pastry wheel, a knife and fork will work just fine, giving the ravioli a rustic, homey look, like the crust on a homemade pie. Try a different shape each time you make ravioli to discover your favorite one.*

Round ravioli (top left)

Use a 2-inch (5-cm) round pastry cutter to make pasta circles. Place 1 teaspoon filling in the center of half the circles. Brush water around the filling, top with the remaining circles, and press the edges to seal.

Half moon–shaped ravioli (left)

Use a 2-inch (5-cm) round pastry cutter to make pasta circles. Place ½ teaspoon filling in the center of each circle. Brush water around the filling, fold in half, and press the edges to seal.

Rustic ravioli (above)

To create crimped edges without a pastry wheel, use a knife to separate the ravioli, then press the edges of each ravioli with a fork to seal.

Ravioli & Tortellini Variations

The most difficult—and most tedious—techniques to master when making ravioli and tortellini are the cutting, shaping, and sealing of the small pasta pillows. With practice, however, these steps become easier, and you'll soon appreciate how fast and satisfying it is to fill and shape your own homemade pasta. Mastering the techniques also means that you will have the basic skills necessary to create a whole new dish by simply substituting the beef filling in the recipe for Ravioli (page 67) or Tortellini (page 75) for one of the following fillings. You can also use a different sauce to add even more variety. Each variation makes 6 to 8 servings.

Cheese Ravioli or Tortellini

A simple blend of three classic cheeses makes a light, yet satisfying filling for ravioli or tortellini.

Follow the recipe for Ravioli (page 67) or Tortellini (page 75), replacing the filling with the one that follows.

To make the cheese filling, in a bowl, whisk together 1½ cups (12 oz/375 g) ricotta cheese, 1 cup (4 oz/125 g) freshly grated Parmigiano-Reggiano cheese, ½ cup (4 oz/125 g) mascarpone cheese, 1 large egg yolk, ⅛ teaspoon freshly grated nutmeg, and ⅛ teaspoon freshly ground pepper until smooth. Cover and chill the filling for at least 1 hour or up to overnight.

Layer the cooked pasta with either Classic Tomato Sauce (page 92) or Tomato Cream Sauce (page 94).

Mushroom Ravioli or Tortellini

This savory mushroom mixture is an ideal filling for vegetarian stuffed pasta. Serve with creamy Alfredo sauce.

Follow the recipe for Ravioli (page 67) or Tortellini (page 75), replacing the filling with the one that follows.

To make the mushroom filling, melt 4 tablespoons (2 oz/60 g) unsalted butter in a large frying pan over medium heat. Add 1 lb (500 g) quartered fresh white mushrooms, 1 teaspoon chopped fresh thyme, 1 teaspoon kosher salt, and ⅛ teaspoon freshly ground pepper and sauté until the juices evaporate and the mushrooms are tender and golden brown, about 10 minutes. Let cool slightly.

Scrape the mixture into a food processor and pulse just until finely chopped. Add ½ cup (4 oz/125 g) ricotta cheese, ½ cup (2 oz/60 g) freshly grated Parmigiano-Reggiano cheese, and 1 large egg yolk. Pulse just until blended, then scrape the mixture into a bowl. Cover and chill the filling for at least 1 hour or up to overnight.

Layer the cooked pasta with Alfredo Sauce (page 55).

Squash Ravioli or Tortellini

Ravioli or tortellini stuffed with butternut squash and tossed with butter and sage sauce are popular in autumn, when winter squashes fill local markets.

Follow the recipe for Ravioli (page 67) or Tortellini (page 75), replacing the filling with the one that follows.

To make the squash filling, preheat the oven to 400°F (200°C) and oil a baking pan. Cut 1 butternut squash (about 2 lb/1 kg) in half lengthwise and discard the seeds. Place the halves, cut side down, in the pan and bake until tender, about 1 hour. Let cool slightly. Scoop the squash flesh into a food processor and discard the skin. Pulse until smooth.

Add 1 cup (4 oz/125 g) freshly grated Parmigiano-Reggiano cheese, 1 large egg, 1 teaspoon kosher salt, ¼ teaspoon freshly grated nutmeg, and ⅛ teaspoon freshly ground pepper to the squash purée. Pulse just until blended, then scrape the mixture into a bowl. Cover and chill the filling for at least 1 hour or up to overnight.

Layer the cooked pasta with Butter & Sage Sauce (page 61).

Chicken Ravioli or Tortellini

Ground chicken seasoned with lemon zest and cheese makes a light filling for ravioli or tortellini.

Follow the recipe for Ravioli (page 67) or Tortellini (page 75), replacing the filling with the one that follows.

To make the chicken filling, warm 2 tablespoons olive oil in a large frying pan over medium heat. Add ½ teaspoon minced garlic and sauté until pale gold and fragrant, about 1 minute. Add 1 lb (500 g) ground (minced) chicken and cook until no trace of pink remains, about 10 minutes.

Using a slotted spoon, transfer the chicken to a food processor. Let the chicken cool slightly, then pulse just until the chicken is finely chopped. Add ½ cup (2 oz/60 g) freshly grated Parmigiano-Reggiano cheese, 1 large egg, 2 tablespoons minced fresh flat-leaf (Italian) parsley, 1 teaspoon grated lemon zest, 1 teaspoon kosher salt, ¼ teaspoon freshly grated nutmeg, and ⅛ teaspoon freshly ground pepper. Pulse just until blended. (Do not pulse too much, or the mixture will become pasty.) Scrape the mixture into a bowl. Cover and chill the filling for at least 1 hour or up to overnight.

Layer the cooked pasta with either Classic Tomato Sauce (page 92) or Tomato Cream Sauce (page 94).

Seafood Ravioli or Tortellini

Shrimp and scallops combine for yet another light filling for ravioli or tortellini. Serve them layered with a creamy tomato sauce and omit the cheese.

Follow the recipe for Ravioli (page 67) or Tortellini (page 75), replacing the filling with the one that follows.

To make the seafood filling, melt 2 tablespoons unsalted butter in a large frying pan over medium heat. Add 2 tablespoons chopped shallot and sauté until tender and golden, 2–3 minutes. Add ½ lb (250 g) peeled and deveined shrimp (prawns), ½ lb (250 g) bay scallops, 1 teaspoon kosher salt, and ⅛ teaspoon freshly ground pepper and cook until the seafood is just barely opaque when cut into at the thickest part, about 2 minutes. Let cool slightly.

Scrape the mixture into a food processor and pulse just until the shrimp and scallops are coarsely chopped. Add 1 tablespoon plain fine dried bread crumbs and pulse just to blend. If the mixture seems wet and soft, pulse in another 1 tablespoon bread crumbs. Add 1 tablespoon minced fresh flat-leaf (Italian) parsley and 1 large egg white and pulse until evenly mixed. Scrape the mixture into a bowl. Cover and chill the filling for at least 1 hour or up to overnight.

Layer the cooked pasta with Tomato Cream Sauce (page 94).

Sausage Ravioli or Tortellini

Sausage makes a bolder, spicier filling than beef for ravioli and tortellini and can be paired with a more assertive marinara sauce.

Follow the recipe for Ravioli (page 67) or Tortellini (page 75), replacing the filling with the one that follows.

To make the sausage filling, warm 2 tablespoons olive oil in a large nonreactive frying pan over medium heat, add 1 minced garlic clove, and sauté until pale gold and fragrant, about 1 minute. Add 1 lb (500 g) sweet Italian pork sausage (casings removed) and cook, stirring to break up the meat, until no trace of pink remains, about 15 minutes.

Using a slotted spoon, transfer the sausage mixture to a food processor. Let cool slightly, then pulse just until the sausage is finely chopped. Add 2 large eggs, 2 tablespoons tomato paste, ½ cup (2 oz/60 g) freshly grated Parmigiano-Reggiano cheese, ½ teaspoon kosher salt, ⅛ teaspoon freshly ground pepper, and a pinch of freshly grated nutmeg and pulse just until blended. Add ¼ cup (1 oz/30 g) plain fine dried bread crumbs and pulse just to combine. Scrape the mixture into a bowl. Cover and chill the filling for at least 1 hour or up to overnight.

Layer the cooked pasta with Marinara Sauce (page 94).

Tortellini

These compact pasta shapes, also called *cappelletti* in some Italian regions, each enclose a biteful of beef filling flavored with red wine and cheese. Boasting a small peaked top, tortellini are simpler to make than they appear, and are easy to learn with a little practice. Here, they are tossed with a creamy tomato sauce.

1 Prepare the ingredients for the filling

If you are not sure how to dice the carrot, celery, and onion, turn to pages 42, 43, and 44. First, dice the carrot: Peel the carrot with a vegetable peeler, then use a chef's knife to cut it into ¼-inch (6-mm) dice. Then, dice the celery: Use the knife to trim the ends of the celery stalk and dice it into the same-sized pieces as the carrot. Finally, dice the onion: Cut the onion in half lengthwise and peel each half. One at a time, place the onion halves, cut side down, on the cutting board. Alternately make a series of lengthwise cuts, parallel cuts, then crosswise cuts to create ¼-inch (6-mm) dice. Stop just short of the root end; this holds the onion together as you cut. After dicing the vegetables, finely grate the cheese using the small grating holes of a box grater-shredder or a rasp grater. Measure out ½ cup (2 oz/60 g) packed grated cheese for the filling and set the remaining cheese aside.

2 Cook the vegetables and beef

Place a large frying pan over medium heat and add the butter. When the butter has melted and the foam begins to subside, add the carrot, celery, and onion. Cook, stirring occasionally with a wooden spoon, until the vegetables are golden and tender, about 15 minutes. Add the ground beef, salt, and pepper and break up the meat into small pieces with the spoon. Stir well and cook until the meat is no longer red and its juices have evaporated, about 10 minutes. Add the wine, bring to a simmer, and cook until the wine evaporates, about 2 minutes. Remove the pan from the heat and let the filling cool slightly.

3 Process the filling

Scrape the filling mixture into a food processor fitted with the metal blade and pulse until finely chopped. Add the eggs and the ½ cup cheese and pulse just until blended. Add the bread crumbs and pulse to blend. Scrape the filling into a bowl. Cover and chill the filling for at least 1 hour or up to overnight. This will help marry the flavors and firm up the filling so it is easier to work with.

4 Adjust the seasonings

To check the seasonings, it's a good idea to fry a small nugget of the filling mixture to get a better sense of how it will taste when it's fully cooked. Heat the olive oil in a small frying pan over medium heat until it appears to shimmer. Place a small spoonful of the filling in the pan and cook until browned on both sides, about 3 minutes. Using tongs, remove the nugget from the pan and transfer to a plate. When the nugget has cooled slightly, taste it and evaluate the seasonings. If you feel it tastes a little bland, mix a small amount of salt or pepper into the remaining filling mixture.

For the beef filling

1 carrot

1 large stalk celery

1 small yellow onion

⅓ lb (155 g) Parmigiano-Reggiano cheese, plus a little extra for serving, if desired

2 tablespoons unsalted butter

¾ lb (375 g) ground (minced) beef sirloin

¾ teaspoon kosher salt

⅛ teaspoon freshly ground pepper

½ cup (4 fl oz/125 ml) dry red wine such as Barbera

2 large eggs

¼ cup (1 oz/30 g) plain fine dried bread crumbs

1 tablespoon olive oil for frying the filling "nugget"

1 batch Fresh Egg Pasta Dough (page 22)

Kosher salt for cooking the pasta

1 batch Tomato Cream Sauce (page 94)

MAKES ABOUT 120 TORTELLINI, OR 6–8 SERVINGS

CHEF'S TIP
Always read the recipe ingredients list before you begin to assemble your mise en place (page 17). For this recipe, note that you will need to have the pasta dough and sauce already made before you begin.

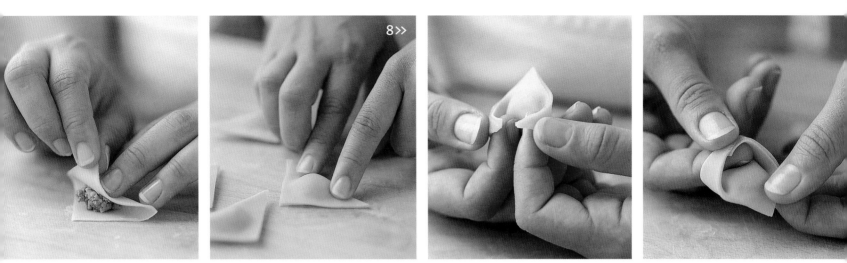

8 >>

5 Knead the dough with a pasta machine

For help with kneading and rolling out fresh pasta dough, turn to page 32. Secure the pasta machine onto your work surface and attach the crank. Cut the dough into 4 equal pieces, then slip 3 of the pieces back under the bowl. Flatten 1 dough piece into a disk about ½ inch (12 mm) thick. Turn the dial on the pasta machine to the widest setting and dust the rollers with flour. Crank the disk through the rollers. Fold the dough into thirds, dust 1 side with flour, and roll it through again. Repeat 8–10 times until the dough is smooth and satiny.

6 Roll out the dough and cut it into squares

Continue passing the dough through the rollers, moving the dial 1 notch narrower after each pass and lightly flouring the dough if it seems sticky (you don't need to fold it at this stage), until it is about ¹⁄₁₆ inch (2 mm) thick, usually after rolling on the second-to-last setting. Trim the rolled-out sheets to create 2-inch (5-cm) squares. Lay the squares flat on a lightly floured rimmed baking sheet, spacing them apart so they don't touch, layering them as needed, and separating the layers with floured lint-free kitchen towels. Repeat steps 5 and 6 with the remaining dough pieces. The pasta squares should not be dried dry before using.

7 Fill the tortellini

Place about ½ teaspoon of the filling in the center of each square. Dip a pastry brush in cool water and lightly brush around the filling; this acts as a glue that keeps the filling tightly sealed inside the pasta. Fold a corner of the dough over the filling to form a triangle.

8 Seal and shape the tortellini

Using your fingers, mold the dough around the filling to eliminate any air pockets. Press the edges of the dough together firmly to seal. Bring the 2 opposite points of the triangle together to form a circle, and pinch the points together to seal. The third point forms a peaked top; curl it back slightly. Place the tortellini, not touching, in a single layer on 2 or 3 lightly floured rimmed baking sheets.

CHEF'S TIP

If you are nervous about making tortellini for the first time, cut out small squares of paper and practice folding and shaping them into the tiny cap shape. Use a glue stick for sealing.

9 Ready your ingredients and equipment for cooking

Since filled pasta takes only a short time to cook and should be served right away, it's a good idea to have everything you need close at hand before cooking it. Preheat the oven to 200°F (95°C) and place a large, shallow serving bowl and individual plates in the oven to warm. Bring a large pot three-fourths full of water to a rolling boil and add about 2 tablespoons salt. While the water is heating, put the Tomato Cream Sauce in a saucepan and bring it to a simmer over medium-low heat. Have ready a colander set over a bowl or in the sink.

CHEF'S TIP

Water will come to a boil faster if the pot is covered. But don't try to jump-start the process by using hot water, as it can carry an off flavor from sitting in the water heater. It's best to start with fresh cold water from the tap.

10 Cook the tortellini

To find out more about cooking fresh filled pasta, turn to page 37. Several at a time, drop half of the tortellini into the boiling water. Reduce the heat slightly so that the water barely simmers. Stir the tortellini gently with a slotted spoon and cook until they rise to the surface. This should only take about 2 minutes. To test the tortellini for doneness, use the slotted spoon to remove 1 tortellini and use a paring knife to cut off one of the edges. Bite into it; the pasta should be tender but still slightly chewy (al dente).

11 Drain and sauce the tortellini

Pour about one-third of the hot sauce into the warmed serving bowl. With the slotted spoon, scoop out the tortellini and place them in the colander to drain for a few seconds. Transfer the drained tortellini to the bowl with the sauce. Spoon on another one-third of the sauce and half of the remaining grated cheese. Cover the bowl with foil to keep the ingredients warm. Turn up the heat so the water returns to a rolling boil. Add the remaining tortellini, reduce the heat to a bare simmer, and cook them as you did the first half. Drain the second batch of tortellini, pour it on top of the first batch, and top with the remaining sauce and cheese.

12 Serve the dish

Using a large spoon, divide the tortellini and sauce among the warmed plates. Sprinkle with more cheese, if desired, and serve right away.

Serving ideas

Tossing tortellini with sauce isn't the only way to enjoy these intricately shaped stuffed pastas. Serving them in brodo (in broth) is another common Italian recipe. Cook the tortellini first, then add them directly to the broth, which can be either plain or laced with eggs and cheese. If you are serving the tortellini with sauce, a few strips of fresh basil or another herb will give it an elegant, colorful, and flavorful garnish.

Tortellini *in brodo* (top left)
This simple soup is often served as a primo, or first course, in Italy. To make it, add a half batch of cooked tortellini to 2 qt (2 l) simmering chicken broth.

Tortellini soup (left)
Inspired by classic Italian *stracciatella*, this soup has fine ribbons of egg and cheese. Whisk together 3 large eggs with ½ cup (2 oz/60 g) freshly grated Parmigiano-Reggiano cheese. Slowly whisk into 2 qt (2 l) simmering chicken broth. Add a half batch of cooked tortellini and top with chopped parsley.

An accent of color (above)
Sprinkling basil cut into a chiffonade (page 39) or minced herbs dresses up many pasta dishes.

Spinach Lasagna

This classic lasagna is built from a hearty, slow-cooked sauce, or *ragù*, a creamy, thick white sauce, and fragrant Parmigiano-Reggiano cheese. The ingredients are placed in the pan in layers, but their flavors come together as the dish is baked. This dish is surprisingly delicate thanks to using tender fresh spinach noodles.

1 Cook and drain the spinach
If you need help making spinach pasta dough, turn to page 24. In a large pot over medium heat, combine the spinach with the water. Cover and cook, stirring occasionally, until the spinach is wilted and tender, 4–5 minutes. Drain in a colander and let cool. Place the spinach in a lint-free kitchen towel and wring it dry.

2 Mix the pasta dough
Add the spinach to a food processor fitted with the metal blade. Break the eggs into a small glass measuring cup and check for shell bits. Pour the eggs into the processor and process until well blended. Add 2 cups (10 oz/315 g) of the flour to the processor and set the remaining ½ cup (2½ oz/75 g) flour nearby. Process until the flour is evenly moistened and crumbly, about 10 seconds. Continue to process, adding the reserved flour 1 tablespoon at a time if the dough seems sticky, for about 30 seconds. A loose ball of dough will form on top of the blade.

3 Lightly knead the dough by hand
Dust a wood or slightly rough plastic work surface and your hands with flour and put the ball of dough in the center of the work surface. Knead the dough until it feels damp but not sticky and is an even green. This will take only a minute or two. Shape the dough into a ball, cover with a large overturned bowl, and let it rest for 30 minutes to relax the gluten.

4 Knead the dough with a pasta machine
For help with kneading and rolling out fresh pasta dough, turn to page 32. Secure the pasta machine onto your work surface and attach the crank. Cut the dough into 4 equal pieces, then slip 3 of the pieces back under the bowl. Flatten 1 dough piece into a disk about ½ inch (12 mm) thick. Turn the dial on the pasta machine to the widest setting and dust the rollers with flour. Crank the disk through the rollers. Fold the dough into thirds, dust 1 side with flour, and roll it through again. Repeat 8–10 times until the dough is smooth and satiny.

5 Roll out the dough into a sheet
Continue passing the dough through the rollers, moving the dial 1 notch narrower after each pass and lightly flouring the dough if it seems sticky (you don't need to fold it at this stage), until it is about 1/16 inch (2 mm) thick. Cut the pasta sheets into sections about 12 inches (30 cm) long (they will get a little longer when cooked). Lay the sections flat on a lightly floured rimmed baking sheet, layering them as needed and separating the layers with floured lint-free kitchen towels. Repeat steps 4 and 5 with the remaining dough pieces. Let dry for 10–20 minutes.

For the spinach pasta dough

1 bunch spinach, about 10 oz (315 g), stemmed and well rinsed

¼ cup (2 fl oz/60 ml) water

3 large eggs

2½ cups (12½ oz/390 g) unbleached all-purpose (plain) flour, plus extra for dusting

For the white sauce

3 cups (24 fl oz/750 ml) whole milk

6 tablespoons (3 oz/90 g) unsalted butter

6 tablespoons (2 oz/60 g) all-purpose (plain) flour

¾ teaspoon kosher salt

Kosher salt for cooking the pasta

6 oz (185 g) Parmigiano-Reggiano cheese, freshly grated to make 1½ cups

1 batch Bolognese Sauce (page 49)

MAKES 8–10 SERVINGS

MAKE-AHEAD TIP
Lasagna can be assembled and then refrigerated, covered tightly, for up to 24 hours before baking. You may need to add as much as 30 minutes to the cooking time. After it has baked for about 1 hour, start checking it every 15 minutes to see if it's ready.

6 Make the white sauce

If you need help making white sauce, turn to page 28. In a small saucepan over medium heat, warm the milk. Place a nonreactive saucepan over medium-low heat and add the butter. When the butter has melted, add the flour and cook, stirring constantly, until the mixture forms a paste, or roux. This should take 2–3 minutes; do not let the roux darken. Remove from the heat and slowly drizzle in the hot milk while whisking constantly. Add the salt, return the pan to medium heat, and cook, stirring constantly, until the sauce is smooth and thick enough to coat the back of a wooden spoon, about 1 minute longer. Remove from the heat.

7 Cook and drain the pasta

Fill a large bowl with ice water and place it near the stove. Bring a large pot three-fourths full of water to a rolling boil and add about 2 tablespoons salt. Add 2 or 3 pasta sections to the water and stir them gently to prevent sticking. Cook, stirring occasionally, until the pasta is tender but still slightly chewy (al dente) when you bite into a small piece cut from a section. This takes only about 1 minute. Using a slotted spoon and skimmer, remove the sections from the pot and place them in the ice water to stop the cooking; this helps prevent the pasta from turning mushy in the oven. Remove the sections from the water and spread them out on lint-free kitchen towels to drain. Cook the remaining pasta sections in the same way.

8 Assemble the lasagna

Position a rack in the middle of the oven and preheat the oven to 375°F (190°C). Butter a 9-by-13-by-2-inch (23-by-33-by-5-cm) baking dish. Set aside the 2 best-looking pasta sections for the top layer, then set aside ½ cup (4 fl oz/125 ml) of the white sauce and ¼ cup (1 oz/30 g) of the cheese for the final topping. Lay 2 sheets of pasta in the buttered dish, overlapping the pieces slightly if needed. Spread the pasta with a thin layer of white sauce, followed by a thin layer of Bolognese sauce, using about ½ cup (4 fl oz/125 ml) of each type of sauce. Sprinkle the Bolognese layer with about ¼ cup (1 oz/30 g) of the cheese. Repeat the layering process, creating 3 or 4 layers with the ingredients. End with the best-looking pasta sections you set aside earlier. (You may have some Bolognese sauce left over.) While you are layering, don't be concerned if some of the pasta sections break, or if you have to cut them to fit the pan. They can be patched together and will not be noticeable when the dish is baked. Spread the top layer with the reserved ½ cup white sauce and sprinkle with the reserved ¼ cup cheese.

9 Bake and serve the lasagna

Bake the lasagna for 40 minutes, then check it. If the top is browning too rapidly, cover the dish loosely with aluminum foil. Continue to bake until the sauce is bubbling around the edges and a knife inserted in the center comes out hot to the touch, 5–15 minutes longer. Remove the dish from the oven, place it on a wire rack, and let it cool for 15 minutes. This allows the lasagna to settle, so that it holds its shape better when cut. Cut the lasagna into squares and serve.

Lasagna Variations

It's easy to create a variety of different lasagnas once you've mastered the classic meat lasagna on page 81. If you want a vegetarian version, replace the Bolognese Sauce with a classic meatless tomato sauce. If you want a lighter dish, double the amount of tomato sauce and omit the White Sauce. Consider savory vegetables such as eggplant or mushrooms and other cheeses such as Fontina or goat cheese, especially for entertaining. You don't need to use spinach noodles, either. In fact, plain noodles are preferable when using additional ingredients with distinctive flavors of their own, such as the Fontina, Ham & Mushroom Lasagna below. Each variation makes 8 to 10 servings.

Vegetarian Lasagna

The sauce for this lasagna is made without meat, making the dish ideal for vegetarians.

Make Fresh Spinach Pasta Dough (page 24) and roll it into 12-inch (30-cm) sections. Next, make 1 batch White Sauce (page 28) and 1 batch Classic Tomato Sauce (page 92). Finally, cook, cool, and drain the pasta sections.

To assemble, preheat the oven to 375°F (190°C). In a buttered 9-by-13-by-2-inch (23-by-33-by-5-cm) baking dish, alternate layers of the pasta with the White Sauce, Classic Tomato Sauce, and 1½ cups (6 oz/185 g) freshly grated Parmigiano-Reggiano cheese. Bake for 45–55 minutes. Let cool for 15 minutes, then cut into squares and serve.

CHEF'S TIP
To avoid confusion when assembling lasagna and other layered dishes, divide the ingredients first and arrange them on the work surface in the order they will be layered.

Eggplant & Goat Cheese Lasagna

Eggplant and creamy cheese pair well in this hearty lasagna.

Make Fresh Spinach Pasta Dough (page 24) and roll it into 12-inch (30 cm) sections. Then, make 2 batches Marinara Sauce (page 94). Next, cut 2 eggplants (aubergines), each about 1 lb (500 g), crosswise into slices ¼ inch (6 mm) thick. Layer the slices in a colander, sprinkle them with kosher salt, and let stand for 30 minutes. Finally, cook, cool, and drain the pasta sections.

Preheat the oven to 400°F (200°C). Rinse the eggplant slices and pat dry. Brush both sides with ⅓ cup (3 fl oz/80 ml) olive oil and arrange in a single layer on baking sheets. Bake, turning once, until tender and lightly browned on both sides, 25–30 minutes total.

To assemble, preheat the oven to 375°F (190°C). In a buttered 9-by-13-by-2-inch (23-by-33-by-5-cm) baking dish, alternate layers of the pasta with the Marinara Sauce, eggplant slices, 2 cups (1 lb/500 g) ricotta cheese, 10 oz (315 g) crumbled fresh goat cheese, and 1 cup (4 oz/125 g) freshly grated Parmigiano-Reggiano cheese. Bake for 45–55 minutes. Let cool for 15 minutes, then cut into squares and serve.

Fontina, Ham & Mushroom Lasagna

This recipe combines mild Fontina, a creamy sauce, and savory ham and mushrooms. Use plain egg pasta instead of spinach pasta.

Make Fresh Egg Pasta Dough (page 22) and roll it into 12-inch (30-cm) sections. Then, make 1 batch White Sauce (page 28). Next, melt 4 tablespoons (2 oz/60 g) unsalted butter in a frying pan over medium heat. Add 1 lb (500 g) sliced fresh white mushrooms, 1 teaspoon kosher salt, and ⅛ teaspoon freshly ground pepper. Sauté until the juices evaporate and the mushrooms are tender and golden brown, about 10 minutes. Finally, cook, cool, and drain the pasta sections.

To assemble, preheat the oven to 375°F (190°C). In a buttered 9-by-13-by-2-inch (23-by-33-by-5-cm) baking dish, alternate layers of the pasta with ½ lb (250 g) chopped cooked ham, the White Sauce, sautéed mushrooms, 2 cups (8 oz/250 g) shredded Fontina Val d'Aosta cheese, and 1 cup (4 oz/125 g) freshly grated Parmigiano-Reggiano cheese. Bake for 45–55 minutes. Let cool for 15 minutes, then cut into squares and serve.

4

Dried Pasta

Made from semolina flour, which lends it a golden color and sturdy texture, dried pasta is the most versatile of all pastas. Here, you will practice cooking dried pasta until it is al dente, the point at which its toothsome qualities reach their height. You will also discover how its hearty flavor can stand up to a robust tomato sauce or pesto, or blend seamlessly with a rich cheese sauce.

Spaghetti & Meatballs

MASTER RECIPE

The secret to making these plump, round meatballs is to brown them well in oil and then cook them at a gentle simmer in the tomato sauce, which keeps the heart of each meatball tender and moist. The thickened sauce also marries well with the spaghetti, easily clinging to the strands.

1 Prepare the ingredients for the meatballs

First, in a small bowl, use a fork to beat the eggs until blended. Then, finely grate the cheese using the small grating holes of a box grater-shredder or a rasp grater. Measure out ½ cup (2 oz/60 g) packed grated cheese and save the remaining cheese for tossing with the pasta later. Finally, mince the garlic and parsley (if you need help, turn to pages 45 and 39): Place the garlic clove on a work surface, firmly press against it with the flat side of a chef's knife, and pull away the papery skin. Use the knife to mince the garlic. Wipe the board and knife clean, then remove the leaves from the parsley sprigs and discard the stems. Using the chef's knife, and holding down the knife tip with one hand, mince the leaves, moving the blade up and down in a rhythmic motion until they are uniformly chopped into very fine pieces. Measure out 3 tablespoons of the minced parsley.

2 Mix the meatballs

In a large bowl, combine the beef, bread crumbs, eggs, cheese, garlic, parsley, salt, and pepper. Using a wooden spoon or your hands, mix together the ingredients just until well blended. Use a light hand when you're doing this, as squeezing the meat mixture too much can result in tough meatballs.

3 Adjust the seasonings

To check the seasonings, it's a good idea to fry a small nugget of the meatball mixture to get a better sense of how it will taste when it's fully cooked. Heat the 1 tablespoon olive oil in a small frying pan over medium heat until it appears to shimmer. Place a small spoonful of the mixture in the pan and cook until browned on both sides, about 3 minutes. Using tongs, remove the nugget from the pan and transfer to a plate. When it has cooled slightly, taste it and evaluate the seasonings. If you feel it tastes a little flat, mix a small amount of salt or pepper into the remaining meat mixture.

4 Portion the meatballs

I find that the easiest way to portion out uniform amounts of the meat mixture is to scoop it up with a spring-action ice cream scoop about 2 inches (5 cm) in diameter. You can also use a ⅓ cup dry measuring cup for this step. As you scoop, place each meatball portion on a rimmed baking sheet lined with parchment (baking) paper. ▸

For the meatballs

2 large eggs

3 oz (90 g) Parmigiano-Reggiano cheese

1 large clove garlic

6–8 sprigs fresh flat-leaf (Italian) parsley

1 lb (500 g) ground (minced) beef

½ cup (2 oz/60 g) plain fine dried bread crumbs

1 teaspoon kosher salt

¼ teaspoon freshly ground pepper

½ cup (4 fl oz/125 ml) olive oil, plus 1 tablespoon for frying the meatball "nugget"

For the sauce

3 tablespoons olive oil

2 cloves garlic, minced (page 45)

2 cans (28 oz/875 g each) Italian peeled tomatoes with juice, chopped

1 teaspoon kosher salt

⅛ teaspoon freshly ground pepper

4 fresh basil leaves

Kosher salt for cooking the pasta

1 lb (500 g) dried spaghetti

MAKES 6–8 SERVINGS

CHEF'S TIP
To make your own dried bread crumbs, dry slices of French or Italian bread on a baking sheet in a 200°F (95°C) oven for about 1 hour. Let the slices cool, break them into small pieces, and then pulse them in a food processor until they form fine crumbs.

5 >

6

5 Shape the meatballs

Moisten your hands with cool water to prevent the mixture from sticking to them and roll each meatball portion between your palms to form a ball. Return the ball to the baking sheet and repeat with the remaining portions, always moistening your hands before you shape each ball. Remember to handle the meat mixture lightly. If you pack or squeeze it, the meatballs could be tough and dry.

6 Brown the meatballs

Place a large sauté pan over medium heat and add the ½ cup olive oil. When the oil appears to shimmer, it is sufficiently hot. Add only as many meatballs to the pan as will fit comfortably without touching one another. (If they are too tightly packed, the meatballs will steam, rather than brown.) Cook the meatballs, turning them frequently with tongs, until they are crusty and dark brown on all surfaces, about 15 minutes total. As the meatballs are ready, transfer them to a plate. Repeat the browning process with the remaining meatballs, letting the pan heat up again slightly between batches. Rinse and dry the sauté pan.

7 Make the sauce

Place the pan over medium heat and add the 3 tablespoons olive oil. When the oil appears to shimmer, add the garlic and cook, stirring often, until it is lightly golden and fragrant, about 2 minutes. Add the tomatoes with their juice, stir in the salt and pepper, and heat until small bubbles begin to form on the surface. Reduce the heat to low and cook, uncovered, until the sauce is thickened, about 20 minutes. Tear the basil leaves into small pieces and stir them into the sauce.

8 Simmer the meatballs in the sauce

Add the meatballs to the sauce and use a large spoon to baste them. Continue to cook over low heat, turning the meatballs occasionally with tongs, until the sauce has thickened and the meatballs are cooked through, about 15 minutes. To check the meatballs for doneness, cut into one; there should be no sign of red at the center. Remove the pan from the heat and cover to keep the meatballs warm.

CHEF'S TIP

Basil turns black when it is chopped and its cut surfaces are exposed to air. To prevent this, many chefs tear the leaves instead, minimizing the darkening effect. I also like the rustic look the rough herb pieces give my sauce.

9 Cook the spaghetti

Preheat the oven to 200°F (95°C); place individual shallow bowls in the oven to warm. For more details on cooking dried pasta, turn to page 38. Bring a large pot three-fourths full of water to a rolling boil and add about 2 tablespoons salt. Add the pasta all at once, stir it gently, and push any strands below the surface of the water if necessary. Let the pasta cook, stirring occasionally, until it is tender but still slightly chewy (al dente), 7–9 minutes. To test it, remove a strand, let it cool slightly, and bite into it; it should show a very thin white line at the core.

CHEF'S TIP

Despite what you may have heard, throwing spaghetti against the wall to see if it sticks is not a good way to test for doneness. Pasta that sticks is surely overdone. Taste a piece instead. With practice, you'll get used to how the texture of the pasta should feel against your teeth. It should be cooked through but still be somewhat chewy.

10 Reheat the meatballs and sauce

A few minutes before you drain the pasta, reheat the sauce and meatballs over low heat until piping hot. Taste the hot sauce and evaluate the seasonings. If the sauce tastes dull, or needs more spice, add more salt and pepper respectively. Mix each seasoning in a little at a time until you achieve a flavor you like.

11 Drain the spaghetti

Transfer 2 ladlefuls of pasta-cooking water to a heatproof container; you'll use it to adjust the consistency of the dish when you toss it. Pour the pasta into a colander to drain, then shake the colander just once to remove some of the water.

12 Toss the spaghetti with the sauce

Using tongs, transfer the meatballs to a plate. Add the drained pasta to the pan with the sauce. Using 2 wooden spoons or spatulas, toss the pasta with the sauce; bring the pasta from the bottom of the pan to the top until all the strands are evenly coated. If the mixture looks dry, add a little of the pasta-cooking water and mix again. Add the reserved cheese and toss again.

13 Serve the dish

Using a pasta fork, divide the sauced pasta evenly among the warmed bowls, using a silicone spatula to scrape out any remaining sauce from the pan. Using tongs, arrange the meatballs on top of the pasta. Serve right away.

Finishing touches

A bowl of spaghetti and meatballs, though normally a casual dish, can be dressed up simply and easily with a sprinkle of bright green herbs or a shower of freshly grated cheese. Both add a bit of color and hint at the delicious flavors to come. You can also serve this favorite American-style dish as they do in Italy, where they split the components and eat them as two separate courses: the sauced pasta first, followed by the meatballs.

Chopped fresh herbs (top left)
A sprinkle of chopped fresh herbs, such as basil (used in the sauce) or parsley (used in the meatballs) adds flavor and color to this or any pasta dish. Simply select an herb already used in the preparation.

Freshly grated cheese (left)
A final sprinkle of Parmigiano-Reggiano cheese will complement most pasta dishes. For the best flavor, always use cheese you have just freshly grated.

Two courses (above)
Rather than arranging the meatballs on top of the tossed pasta, keep them warm while you enjoy the pasta as a first course. Then, bring out the meatballs to serve as the main course.

Pasta with Classic Tomato Sauce

Cooking the carrots, onion, and celery in butter, a sauce base known as a *soffrito* in Italy, lends this simple sauce a mild, sweet flavor. But the main component is still tomato, which means using vine-ripened plum tomatoes in summer and the best-quality canned tomatoes the rest of the year.

For the classic tomato sauce

4 tablespoons (2 oz/60 g) unsalted butter

2 carrots, peeled and finely diced (page 42)

1 small stalk celery, finely diced (page 43)

1 small yellow onion, finely diced (page 44)

2 lb (1 kg) plum (Roma) tomatoes, peeled, seeded, and diced (pages 40–41), or 1 can (28 oz/875 g) Italian peeled tomatoes, drained and chopped

1 teaspoon kosher salt

⅛ teaspoon freshly ground pepper

Kosher salt for cooking the pasta

1 lb (500 g) dried penne

10 fresh basil leaves, torn into small pieces

1 tablespoon unsalted butter

2 oz (60 g) Parmigiano-Reggiano cheese, freshly grated

MAKES 4–6 SERVINGS

CHEF'S TIP

Italian cooks aren't shy about using canned tomatoes for sauce when fresh tomatoes are not in season. You can find the same imported Italian peeled tomatoes they use at specialty-food stores and well-stocked markets.

1 **Make the *soffrito* for the sauce**
Place a 12-inch (30-cm) frying pan over medium heat and add the 4 tablespoons butter. When the butter has melted and the foam begins to subside, add the carrots, celery, and onion. Cook, stirring occasionally, until the onion is translucent and the carrots and celery are very tender, about 15 minutes. Adjust the heat if necessary so that the vegetables do not brown, which would make the sauce bitter. Stir in a spoonful of warm water to slow the cooking if needed.

2 **Simmer the sauce**
Add the tomatoes, salt, and pepper and cook until the sauce begins to bubble. Reduce the heat to the lowest setting and cook, stirring occasionally, until the sauce is thickened and the tomato juices have evaporated, about 20 minutes. Taste the sauce. If you feel it tastes bland, stir in a bit more salt or pepper to brighten the flavors. Remove the pan from the heat.

3 **Cook and drain the penne**
Preheat the oven to 200°F (95°C) and place individual plates in the oven to warm. Bring a large pot three-fourths full of water to a rolling boil and add about 2 tablespoons salt. Add the pasta all at once and stir it gently. Let the pasta cook, stirring occasionally, until it is tender but still slightly chewy (al dente) and shows a very thin white line at the core when you bite into it, 7–9 minutes. While the pasta is cooking, reheat the sauce over medium-low heat. Transfer 2 ladlefuls of pasta-cooking water to a heatproof container; you'll use it to adjust the consistency of the dish when you toss it. Pour the pasta into a colander to drain, then shake the colander just once to remove some of the remaining water. The pasta should still be moist.

4 **Toss the penne with the sauce**
Add the drained pasta to the pan with the sauce and, using a wooden spoon or spatula, stir and toss the pasta until it is well coated with the sauce. If the mixture looks dry as you toss, drizzle a little of the reserved pasta-cooking water over the pasta and continue to toss. The pasta should be evenly coated with the sauce. Add the basil and the 1 tablespoon butter and toss to distribute evenly. (The butter gives the sauce a creamy finish.) Remove the pan from the heat, add the cheese, and toss again to coat evenly.

5 **Serve the dish**
Using a large serving spoon, divide the sauced pasta evenly among the warmed plates. Serve right away.

Tomato Sauce Variations

You may be surprised to learn how many types of sauces you can make using either fresh tomatoes or canned tomatoes, depending on the season. Among them are the six traditional Italian favorites that follow, each made from just a handful of good-quality ingredients. Mix and match the sauces with almost any dried pasta shape you like, from penne and farfalle to linguine and *bucatini;* the latter is a classic partner for *amatriciana* sauce. For more information on pairing pasta and sauces, turn to page 18. Keep your pantry stocked with tomato-sauce basics, and you will be able to make any of these classics at a moment's notice. Each variation makes 4 to 6 servings.

Pasta with Tomato Cream Sauce

The addition of cream to a tomato sauce provides richness while cutting the tartness of the tomatoes.

Follow the recipe to make Classic Tomato Sauce (page 92). In step 2, once the sauce has thickened, stir in ½ cup (4 fl oz/ 125 ml) heavy (double) cream and simmer for 5 minutes longer. Remove the pan from the heat and adjust the seasonings.

Cook 1 lb (500 g) dried penne or other pasta for 7–9 minutes, reserve some of the cooking water, and drain the pasta. Toss the pasta with the sauce until evenly coated, adjusting the consistency with the cooking water. Serve right away.

Pasta with Fresh Tomato Sauce

This simple uncooked sauce, which features summertime's vine-ripened tomatoes and fresh basil, is a perfect recipe for a hot day.

To make the sauce, in a large bowl, mix together 2 lb (1 kg) peeled, seeded, and diced plum (Roma) tomatoes; ¼ cup (⅓ oz/10 g) chopped fresh basil; 1 minced garlic clove; ¼ cup (2 fl oz/60 ml) extra-virgin olive oil; 1 teaspoon kosher salt; and ¼ teaspoon freshly ground pepper. Let the mixture stand for 30 minutes.

Cook 1 lb (500 g) dried penne or other pasta for 7–9 minutes, reserve some of the cooking water, and drain the pasta. Transfer the pasta to a warmed serving bowl, add the sauce, and toss until the pasta is well coated, adjusting the consistency with the cooking water. If desired, add ½ cup (2 oz/60 g) freshly grated Parmigiano-Reggiano cheese and toss again. Serve right away.

Pasta with Marinara Sauce

Marinara sauce differs from Classic Tomato Sauce because it starts with olive oil and garlic instead of a *soffrito*. It is a slightly more assertive sauce that can stand on its own, or pair with equally assertive ingredients.

To make the sauce, in a 12-inch (30-cm) nonreactive frying pan over medium heat, warm ¼ cup (2 fl oz/60 ml) olive oil. Add 2 minced garlic cloves and sauté until lightly golden, about 2 minutes. Add 1 can (28 oz/875 g) drained and chopped Italian peeled tomatoes, 1 teaspoon kosher salt, and ¼ teaspoon freshly ground pepper. Bring to a simmer, reduce the heat to low, and cook until thickened, about 20 minutes. Remove the pan from the heat and adjust the seasonings.

Cook 1 lb (500 g) dried penne or other pasta for 7–9 minutes, reserve some of the cooking water, and drain the pasta. Toss the pasta with the sauce until evenly coated, adjusting the consistency with the cooking water. Add 6 torn fresh basil leaves and toss well. If desired, add ½ cup (2 oz/60 g) freshly grated Parmigiano-Reggiano cheese and toss again. Serve right away.

Pasta with Arrabbiata Sauce

Arrabbiata means "angry" in Italian and refers to the red pepper flakes used to flavor the sauce.

To make the sauce, in a 12-inch (30-cm) nonreactive frying pan over medium heat, warm ¼ cup (2 fl oz/60 ml) olive oil. Add 2 minced garlic cloves and ½ teaspoon red pepper flakes and sauté until lightly golden, about 2 minutes. Add 1 can (28 oz/875 g) drained and chopped Italian peeled tomatoes and 1 teaspoon kosher salt. Bring to a simmer, reduce the heat to low, and cook until thickened, about 20 minutes. Remove the pan from the heat and adjust the seasonings.

Cook 1 lb (500 g) dried penne or other pasta for 7–9 minutes, reserve some of the cooking water, and drain the pasta. Toss the pasta with the sauce until evenly coated, adjusting the consistency with the cooking water. Serve right away.

CHEF'S TIP

During tomato season (June through September), use 2 lb (1 kg) peeled, seeded, and diced fresh plum (Roma) tomatoes (pages 40–41) instead of the canned ones in the recipes for marinara, arrabbiata, puttanesca, and amatriciana sauce.

Pasta with Amatriciana Sauce

Amatriciana sauce features pancetta, onions, and red pepper flakes in a hearty, spicy tomato sauce.

To make the sauce, in a 12-inch (30-cm) nonreactive frying pan over medium heat, warm 2 tablespoons olive oil. Add 1 diced small yellow onion, 2 oz (60 g) diced pancetta, and ¼ teaspoon red pepper flakes. Sauté until the onion is golden and tender and the pancetta is lightly golden, about 15 minutes. Stir in 1 can (28 oz/875 g) drained and chopped Italian peeled tomatoes and 1 teaspoon kosher salt. Bring to a simmer, reduce the heat to low, and cook until thickened, about 20 minutes. Remove the pan from the heat and adjust the seasonings.

Cook 1 lb (500 g) dried penne or other pasta for 7–9 minutes, reserve some of the cooking water, and drain the pasta. Toss the pasta with the sauce until evenly coated, adjusting the consistency with the cooking water. If desired, add ½ cup (2 oz/60 g) freshly grated *pecorino romano* or Parmigiano-Reggiano cheese and toss again. Serve right away.

Pasta with Puttanesca Sauce

Puttanesca sauce incorporates the piquant flavors of olives, anchovies, and capers into the tomato sauce.

To make the sauce, in a 12-inch (30-cm) nonreactive frying pan over medium heat, warm ¼ cup (2 fl oz/60 ml) olive oil. Add 2 minced garlic cloves and ½ teaspoon red pepper flakes and sauté until lightly golden, about 2 minutes. Add 1 can (28 oz/875 g) drained and chopped Italian peeled tomatoes, 1 teaspoon kosher salt, and ¼ teaspoon freshly ground black pepper. Bring to a simmer, reduce the heat to low, and cook until thickened, about 20 minutes. Add 6–8 chopped olive oil–packed anchovy fillets, ¼ cup (1½ oz/45 g) chopped pitted Gaeta or Kalamata olives, 2 tablespoons chopped drained capers, and 2 tablespoons chopped fresh flat-leaf (Italian) parsley and simmer for about 1 minute longer. Remove the pan from the heat and adjust the seasonings.

Cook 1 lb (500 g) dried penne or other pasta for 7–9 minutes, reserve some of the cooking water, and drain the pasta. Toss the pasta with the sauce until evenly coated, adjusting the consistency with the cooking water. Serve right away.

Linguine Aglio Olio

Named after its primary ingredients, *aglio* (garlic) and *olio* (oil), this simple pasta dish depends on using the very best quality extra-virgin olive oil you can afford. Without it, the naturally bold flavors of garlic and red pepper flakes will dominate, rather than blend with, the oil that forms the base of the sauce.

1 **Thinly slice the garlic**
If you are not sure how to work with garlic, turn to page 45. Working with 1 garlic clove at a time, place a clove on a work surface and press against it firmly with the flat side of the chef's knife; the papery skin will split. Try not to smash the clove too much; you want to keep the clove relatively intact. Peel away the garlic skin, then cut the clove in half lengthwise. If you see a small green sprout at the center, use the tip of a paring knife to pop it out of the clove; these can be bitter. Switch back to the chef's knife and thinly slice the garlic halves lengthwise. Repeat the peeling and slicing processes with the remaining garlic cloves, then set the garlic aside.

2 **Mince the parsley**
If you need help mincing parsley, turn to page 39. Remove the leaves from the parsley sprigs and discard the stems. Place the leaves on a cutting board. Using a chef's knife, and holding down the knife tip with one hand, mince the leaves, moving the blade up and down in a rhythmic motion until they are uniformly chopped into very fine pieces. Measure out ⅓ cup (½ oz/15 g) of the minced parsley.

3 **Make the sauce**
Place a 12-inch (30-cm) frying pan over medium-low heat and add the olive oil. When the oil appears to shimmer, it is sufficiently hot. Add the garlic and red pepper flakes and cook, stirring often, until the garlic is golden and fragrant, 4–5 minutes. Adjust the heat as needed to make sure that the ingredients do not burn. If they scorch, they will impart a bitter flavor to the sauce. Stir in the parsley and remove the pan from the heat.

4 **Cook the linguine**
Preheat the oven to 200°F (95°C) and place individual shallow bowls in the oven to warm. For more details on cooking dried pasta, turn to page 38. Bring a large pot three-fourths full of water to a rolling boil and add about 2 tablespoons salt. Add the pasta all at once and stir it gently to prevent sticking. Push any strands below the surface of the water if necessary. Let the pasta cook, stirring occasionally, until it is tender but still slightly chewy (al dente), 7–9 minutes. To test it, use tongs to remove a strand, let it cool slightly, and bite into it; it should show a very thin white line at the core. While the pasta is cooking, reheat the sauce over medium-low heat.

6 large cloves garlic

12 sprigs fresh flat-leaf (Italian) parsley

⅓ cup (3 fl oz/80 ml) extra-virgin olive oil

½ teaspoon red pepper flakes

Kosher salt for cooking the pasta

1 lb (500 g) dried linguine

MAKES 4–6 SERVINGS

CHEF'S TIP
Don't be tempted to use fresh pasta for this dish. Olive oil–based sauces are better suited for dried pasta. They readily coat its lightly textured surface without being absorbed by it.

5 Drain the linguine

Transfer 2 ladlefuls of pasta-cooking water to a heatproof container; you'll use it to adjust the consistency of the dish when you toss it. Pour the pasta into a colander to drain, then shake the colander just once to remove some of the remaining water. The pasta should still be moist.

6 Adjust the seasonings

Taste the warmed sauce and evaluate the seasonings. You may want to add a bit of salt, as the only salt in the dish will come from the pasta-cooking water. It you crave a spicier dish, add a few more red pepper flakes. Mix in any seasonings a little bit at a time and taste the dish again until you are happy with the flavors.

7 Toss the linguine with the sauce

Add the drained pasta to the pan with the sauce. Using 2 wooden spoons or spatulas, toss the ingredients together; bring the pasta from the bottom of the pan to the top until all the strands are evenly coated with the sauce. To do this thoroughly, plan on about 30 seconds of tossing. If the mixture looks dry as you toss, drizzle a little of the reserved pasta-cooking water over the pasta and continue to toss. The parsley and garlic should be evenly distributed throughout, and each strand of linguine should be glistening with oil.

8 Serve the dish

Using a pasta fork, divide the sauced pasta evenly among the warmed bowls, using a silicone spatula to scrape out any remaining sauce from the pan. To create the attractive coils of pasta shown on page 96, use a large fork to pick up a generous amount of the pasta and twirl it against the base of a large metal spoon. Transfer the coil to a bowl and repeat with the remaining pasta. Serve right away.

CHEF'S TIP

To release more heat from the red pepper flakes, crush them lightly in a mortar with a pestle, or between your fingers, before adding the flakes to the sauce.

Olive Oil–Based Sauce Variations

Once you've learned how to make a simple pan sauce based on olive oil and a few select ingredients, as demonstrated in Linguine Aglio Olio (page 97), you will have in your repertory a basic technique that accommodates many other ingredients. This style of cooking pasta is from southern Italy, where recipes based on olive oil and dried pasta have long been traditional. The possibilities for flavorful blends and interesting pasta shapes this region has inspired are countless. After you've tried the three variations that appear here, you will feel fully confident to experiment with new shapes and sauce combinations of your own. Each variation makes 4 to 6 servings.

Linguine with Clam Sauce

This dish is popular year-round along Italy's long coastline.

Scrub 4 lb (2 kg) Manila or other small hard-shell clams. Discard any that do not close to the touch. In a large pot over medium-high heat, combine the clams and ¼ cup (2 fl oz/60 ml) water. Cover, bring to a boil, and cook until the clam shells just open, 3–4 minutes. Transfer to a bowl, discarding any that failed to open. Strain the broth through a sieve lined with cheesecloth (muslin) into a clean bowl. Remove the clams from their shells and put them in another bowl.

In a large frying pan over medium-low heat, warm ⅓ cup (3 fl oz/80 ml) extra-virgin olive oil. When hot, add 6 sliced large garlic cloves and ½ teaspoon red pepper flakes and sauté until the garlic is golden, 4–5 minutes. Add the clam juice and cook until slightly reduced, about 1 minute. Remove from the heat and stir in ⅓ cup (½ oz/15 g) minced fresh flat-leaf (Italian) parsley and the clams.

Cook 1 lb (500 g) dried linguine for 7–9 minutes, reserve some of the cooking water, and drain the pasta. Toss the pasta with the sauce until evenly coated, adjusting the consistency with the cooking water. Serve right away.

Farfalle with Mushrooms, Garlic & Parsley

Here, fresh mushrooms are added to the original sauce, while a classic short pasta—bow tie–shaped farfalle—replaces the long, slender linguine.

In a large frying pan over medium-low heat, warm ⅓ cup (3 fl oz/80 ml) extra-virgin olive oil. When hot, add 6 sliced large garlic cloves and ½ teaspoon red pepper flakes and sauté until the garlic is pale gold and fragrant, 2–3 minutes. Raise the heat to medium and add 1 lb (500 g) sliced assorted fresh mushrooms such as oyster, shiitake, and white button. Sauté until the mushroom juices evaporate and the mushrooms are golden brown, about 10 minutes. Stir in ⅓ cup (½ oz/15 g) minced fresh flat-leaf (Italian) parsley.

Cook 1 lb (500 g) dried farfalle for 7–9 minutes, reserve some of the cooking water, and drain the pasta. Toss the pasta with the sauce until evenly coated, adjusting the consistency with the cooking water. Serve right away.

Whole-Wheat Penne with Summer Vegetables

In early summer, I make a hearty pan sauce of garden-fresh vegetables quickly cooked in the garlic-laced olive oil. Nutty whole-wheat pasta, such as whole-wheat penne, works well for this preparation.

In a large frying pan over medium-low heat, warm ⅓ cup (3 fl oz/80 ml) extra-virgin olive oil. When hot, add 6 sliced large garlic cloves, 2 sliced zucchini (courgettes), ½ lb (250 g) bite-sized asparagus pieces, 1 teaspoon kosher salt, and ½ teaspoon red pepper flakes. Sauté until the vegetables are almost tender, about 4 minutes. Add 1 cup (6 oz/185 g) halved cherry tomatoes, ½ teaspoon dried oregano, and freshly ground pepper to taste. Cook until the tomatoes have just begun to collapse, about 3 minutes.

Cook 1 lb (500 g) dried whole-wheat (wholemeal) penne for 7–9 minutes, reserve some of the cooking water, and drain the pasta. Toss the pasta with the sauce until evenly coated, adjusting the consistency with the cooking water. Serve right away.

Penne with Pesto, Potatoes & Green Beans

At its best, pesto is a beautiful emerald green and still has a bit of texture. In Italy, it is traditionally paired with *trenette*, a fresh ribbon pasta, but it also goes well with dried pasta. Green beans and new potatoes are classic partners, making this a perfect dish for early summer when the vegetables and herbs are at their peak.

1 Make the pesto
Put the basil, pine nuts, garlic, and salt in a large mortar. Using a pestle, and working in a circular motion, grind the ingredients together until a dense, thick green paste forms. This could take several minutes to do, but don't be discouraged. Slowly drizzle in the olive oil while stirring continuously with the pestle until a thick, flowing sauce forms. Transfer the mixture to a bowl and then use a spoon to stir in the cheese. Taste the pesto; it should taste primarily of fresh basil with accents of garlic, nuts, and cheese. If you feel it tastes bland, stir in more cheese or salt until the flavors are nicely balanced. Keep in mind that the flavor will be diluted once it is mixed with the pasta and vegetables.

2 Cook the vegetables
Preheat the oven to 200°F (95°C) and place a large, shallow bowl and individual plates in the oven to warm. Bring a large pot three-fourths full of water to a rolling boil and add about 2 tablespoons salt. Add the potatoes and green beans and cook until tender, about 5 minutes. Use a large slotted spoon to transfer the potatoes and beans to the warmed large bowl. Cover the bowl lightly with aluminum foil to keep the vegetables warm.

3 Cook and drain the penne
Bring the water back to a rolling boil, add the pasta all at once, and stir it gently. Let the pasta cook, stirring occasionally, until it is tender but still slightly chewy (al dente), 7–9 minutes. (For more details on cooking dried pasta, turn to page 38.) Transfer 2 ladlefuls of pasta-cooking water to a heatproof container; you'll use it to adjust the consistency of the dish when you toss it. Pour the pasta into a colander to drain, then shake the colander just once to remove some of the remaining water. The pasta should still be moist.

4 Toss the penne with the sauce and vegetables
Add the drained pasta to the bowl with the vegetables and then add the pesto. Using a wooden spoon or spatula, stir and toss the pasta and vegetables until they are well coated with the sauce. If the mixture looks dry, add a little of the pasta-cooking water and mix again. Add the butter and toss to coat evenly.

5 Serve the dish
Using a large serving spoon, divide the sauced pasta and vegetables evenly among the warmed plates. Serve right away.

For the pesto

1½ cups (1½ oz/45 g) lightly packed fresh basil leaves

3 tablespoons pine nuts

1 clove garlic, coarsely chopped (page 45)

½ teaspoon kosher salt

⅓ cup (3 fl oz/80 ml) extra-virgin olive oil

¼ lb (125 g) Parmigiano-Reggiano cheese, freshly grated

Kosher salt for cooking the vegetables and the pasta

½ lb (250 g) small red potatoes, peeled and sliced about ¼ inch (6 mm) thick

½ lb (250 g) young, thin green beans, stem ends trimmed

1 lb (500 g) dried penne

1 tablespoon unsalted butter, at room temperature

MAKES 4–6 SERVINGS

CHEF'S TIP
To keep pesto a vibrant green, many chefs add a couple tablespoons of flat-leaf (Italian) parsley leaves to their formula. Parsley doesn't darken the way basil does when it is pounded or cut.

¼ lb (125 g) thick-cut pancetta or lightly smoked bacon slices (⅛ inch/3 mm thick)

1 tablespoon olive oil

3 large eggs

½ teaspoon kosher salt

¼ teaspoon freshly ground pepper

Kosher salt for cooking the pasta

1 lb (500 g) dried spaghetti

3 oz (90 g) *pecorino romano* cheese, freshly grated, plus a little extra for serving

MAKES 6 MAIN-COURSE SERVINGS OR 8 FIRST-COURSE SERVINGS

CHEF'S TIP
If you have time, put the pancetta in the freezer for about 15 minutes before you begin the recipe; it is easier to cut when it's partially frozen.

Spaghetti Carbonara

This Roman pasta dish combines a pale yellow sauce made from fresh eggs and sharp pecorino cheese with crisp bits of pleasantly salty pancetta. Since the recipe relies on just a few items, it is especially important to use fresh, high-quality ingredients. Note that this recipe includes partially cooked eggs. For more details, see page 137.

1 Prepare the pancetta
Stack the pancetta slices on a cutting board. Using a chef's knife, cut the stack into strips ¼ inch (6 mm) wide. Then, make a second series of ¼-inch cuts perpendicular to the first cuts to create ¼-inch dice. Place a 12-inch (30-cm) frying pan over medium heat and add the olive oil. When the oil appears to shimmer, add the pancetta and stir to separate the pieces. Cook, stirring occasionally, until the pancetta is lightly golden around the edges, about 10 minutes. Remove the pan from the heat. Don't be tempted to pour off the fat at this point; it adds wonderful flavor to the dish and helps create a creamy sauce.

2 Beat the eggs
Break the eggs into a bowl and check carefully to make sure they are free of shell bits. Add the salt and pepper. Using a fork, beat the mixture until blended.

3 Cook and drain the spaghetti
Preheat the oven to 200°F (95°C) and place individual shallow bowls in the oven to warm. Bring a large pot three-fourths full of water to a rolling boil and add about 2 tablespoons salt. Add the pasta all at once, stir it gently, and push any strands below the surface of the water if necessary. Let the pasta cook, stirring occasionally, until it is tender but still slightly chewy (al dente), 7–9 minutes. To test it, use tongs to remove a strand, let it cool slightly, and bite into it; it should show a very thin white line at the core. While the pasta is cooking, reheat the pancetta over medium heat until you hear it sizzle. Transfer 2 ladlefuls of pasta-cooking water to a heatproof container. Pour the pasta into a colander to drain, then shake the colander just once to remove some of the remaining water.

4 Toss the spaghetti with the sauce
Add the drained pasta to the pan with the pancetta and, using 2 wooden spoons or spatulas, stir and toss the pasta until the pancetta is distributed evenly. Add the egg mixture and about 2 tablespoons of the pasta-cooking water and toss again until the mixture looks creamy, adding a little more water if needed. Be sure to toss steadily and quickly so that the eggs form a creamy sauce, rather than scramble. This should take about 30 seconds. Remove the pan from the heat, sprinkle the pasta with the cheese, and toss again to distribute the cheese evenly.

5 Serve the dish
Using a pasta fork, divide the sauced pasta evenly among the warmed bowls. It's hard to adjust the seasonings for this dish ahead of time, so pass freshly ground pepper and extra cheese at the table. Serve right away.

Baked Ziti with Ricotta, Mozzarella, Sausage & Tomato Sauce

As you mix the sauce and sausages with the ziti (short, sturdy pasta tubes), they not only coat the pasta, but are also trapped inside their hollows, delivering a burst of flavor with each bite. The ricotta and mozzarella cheeses give this rustic, substantial dish a pleasing creamy quality.

1 Cook the sausages
Place the sausages in a single layer in a frying pan and add water to reach halfway up their sides. Place the pan over medium heat until the water bubbles gently, and cook until the water evaporates, about 5 minutes. Continue cooking the sausages, turning them frequently, until they are cooked through and nicely browned on all sides, about 10 minutes longer. Transfer the sausages to a cutting board and cut crosswise into slices ¼ inch (6 mm) thick.

2 Cook the ziti
While the sausages are cooking, position a rack in the middle of the oven and preheat the oven to 350°F (180°C). Bring a large pot three-fourths full of water to a rolling boil and add about 2 tablespoons salt. Add the pasta all at once and stir it gently to prevent sticking. Let the pasta cook, stirring occasionally, until it is almost tender but still slightly undercooked when you bite into it, 6–8 minutes. The pasta will cook further when it is baked.

3 Drain and sauce the ziti
Pour the pasta into a colander to drain, then shake the colander just once to remove some of the remaining water. The pasta should still be moist. Return the pasta to the pot. Add the sausages, half of the marinara sauce, and ½ cup (2 oz/60 g) of the grated Parmigiano-Reggiano cheese and stir and toss well to mix evenly.

4 Layer the ingredients in a baking dish
Spread half the pasta and sausage mixture in a 9-by-13-by-2-inch (23-by-33-by-5-cm) baking dish. Drop spoonfuls of the ricotta evenly over the top. Sprinkle the entire surface evenly with the mozzarella. Pour about 1 cup (8 fl oz/250 ml) of the remaining sauce evenly over the mozzarella. Top with the remaining pasta and sausage mixture and then the remaining sauce. Sprinkle with the remaining ½ cup grated Parmigiano-Reggiano cheese.

5 Bake and serve the dish
Cover tightly with aluminum foil and bake for 45 minutes. Uncover and continue to bake until the sauce is bubbling around the edges and a knife inserted into the center comes out hot to the touch, about 15 minutes longer. (If the top seems to be browning too fast, re-cover the dish loosely with foil and continue to bake.) Remove the dish from the oven, cover it loosely with foil, and let it cool on a wire rack for about 15 minutes. Scoop out portions with a large metal spoon.

---

1 lb (500 g) sweet Italian pork sausages

Kosher salt for cooking the pasta

1 lb (500 g) dried ziti

2 batches Marinara Sauce (page 94)

¼ lb (125 g) Parmigiano-Reggiano cheese, freshly grated to make 1 cup

2 cups (1 lb/500 g) whole-milk or part-skim ricotta cheese

¾ lb (375 g) fresh mozzarella cheese, drained and shredded to make 3 cups

MAKES 8–10 SERVINGS

MAKE-AHEAD TIP
This dish can be assembled and then refrigerated, tightly covered, for up to 24 hours before baking. When baking, you may need to add as much as 30 minutes to the cooking time. After it has baked for about 1 hour, start checking it every 15 minutes to see if it's ready.

Baked Macaroni & Cheese

In this family favorite, golden yellow sharp Cheddar cheese is melted into a thick white sauce, then mixed with elbow macaroni or pasta shells. I like to bake my version of this traditional recipe in a shallow baking dish with a sprinkle of bread crumbs scattered over the surface. The beautifully browned, crisp topping is the perfect contrast to the tender, cheese-coated pasta below.

1 batch White Sauce (page 28)

⅛ teaspoon freshly grated nutmeg

⅛ teaspoon freshly ground white pepper

½ lb (250 g) sharp Cheddar or Gruyère cheese, freshly shredded to make 2 cups

Kosher salt for cooking the pasta

1 lb (500 g) dried elbow macaroni or small shells (conchiglie)

2 tablespoons plain dried bread crumbs

MAKES 6 MAIN-COURSE SERVINGS OR
12 SIDE-DISH SERVINGS

MAKE-AHEAD TIP

This dish can be assembled and then refrigerated, tightly covered, for up to 24 hours before baking. When baking, you may need to add as much as 30 minutes to the cooking time. After it has baked for about 30 minutes, start checking it every 10 minutes to see if it's ready.

1 **Reheat the sauce if necessary**
If you have just made the White Sauce, proceed to step 2. If you have made the sauce in advance, pour it into a heavy-bottomed saucepan, place over low heat, and stir constantly with a wooden spoon or whisk until the sauce begins to bubble. Add a little hot water to thin it, if necessary.

2 **Stir the cheese into the sauce**
Remove the sauce from the heat and stir in the nutmeg and pepper. Add 1½ cups (6 oz/185 g) of the cheese and stir until melted. Don't worry if the cheese doesn't melt completely or the sauce looks streaked; the cheese will continue to melt as it bakes. Taste the sauce and evaluate the seasonings. If the sauce tastes dull or needs more spice, stir in a bit of salt, nutmeg, or pepper a little at a time until you achieve a flavor you like. Note, however, that the flavor will mellow slightly when the sauce is mixed with the pasta. Cover the sauce with a piece of plastic wrap, pressing it directly onto the surface to prevent a skin from forming.

3 **Cook and drain the macaroni**
Position a rack in the middle of the oven and preheat the oven to 400°F (200°C). Butter a 9-by-13-by-2-inch (23-by-33-by-5-cm) baking dish. Bring a large pot three-fourths full of water to a rolling boil and add about 2 tablespoons salt. Add the pasta all at once and stir it gently to prevent sticking. Let the pasta cook, stirring occasionally, until it is almost tender, but still slightly undercooked when you bite into it, 6–8 minutes. The pasta will cook further when it is baked. Pour the pasta into a colander to drain, then shake the colander just once to remove some of the remaining water. The pasta should still be moist.

4 **Layer the ingredients in a baking dish**
Immediately return the pasta to the pot, add the cheese sauce, and stir to coat the pasta evenly with the sauce. With a silicone spatula, scrape the pasta and cheese into the prepared baking dish. Sprinkle the sauced pasta evenly with the remaining ½ cup (2 oz/60 g) cheese, and then with the bread crumbs.

5 **Bake and serve the dish**
Bake until the sauce is bubbling around the edges, the top is nicely browned, and a knife inserted into the center comes out hot to the touch, about 30 minutes. (If the top seems to be browning too fast, cover the dish loosely with aluminum foil and continue to bake.) Transfer the dish to a wire rack and let cool for about 5 minutes before serving. Scoop out portions with a large metal spoon.

5

Noodles & Dumplings

In addition to its many pasta dishes, Italy has several dumplings of its own, the best-known being potato-based gnocchi. Recipes for other pastalike noodles and dumplings are found in cuisines worldwide, particularly in Asia, such as buckwheat-based soba noodles and pot stickers. In this chapter, you will learn about these and other international traditions for preparing noodles and dumplings.

Gnocchi Gratin

In this simple gratin, handmade potato dumplings are blanketed with a velvety white sauce and then topped with Parmigiano-Reggiano cheese and bread crumbs. During baking the crust turns golden brown and crisp, forming an appealing contrast to the light dumplings and creamy sauce.

1 Bake the potatoes

Position a rack in the middle of the oven and preheat the oven to 350°F (180°C). Using the tines of a fork, prick the potatoes once or twice about ¼ inch (6 mm) deep. This allows them to release steam as they bake, so the potato flesh is fairly dry when they finish cooking. Place the potatoes directly on the oven rack and bake until the flesh is very tender when pierced with a small knife, about 1½ hours. Using pot holders, remove the potatoes from the oven and set them on the counter to cool.

2 "Rice" the potatoes

When the potatoes are just cool enough to handle, cut them in half lengthwise. Using a large metal spoon, scoop out the potato flesh from the skins. Fit a ricer or a food mill with the disk with the small holes. Force the potato flesh through the ricer or mill, allowing it to fall onto a large, rimmed baking sheet. Using a heatproof silicone spatula, spread out the potato flesh on the sheet and let it cool completely. This step allows excess moisture to evaporate, so that the potatoes are as dry as possible when you make the dough.

3 Make the gnocchi dough

Break the eggs into a bowl and check for shell bits. Add the salt and beat the eggs with a fork until blended. When the potatoes are completely cool, drizzle them evenly with the egg mixture. Then, sprinkle 1 cup (5 oz/155 g) of the flour evenly over the potatoes. Using a bench scraper, scoop, lift, and fold the potatoes to mix them with the eggs and flour until a coarse dough forms. It should look raggedy. Mixing the dough this way, by hand, helps keep the texture of the gnocchi light and delicate. ›

For the gnocchi

5 russet potatoes, about 2½ lb (1.25 kg) total weight

2 large eggs

1 teaspoon kosher salt

2 cups (10 oz/315 g) unbleached all-purpose (plain) flour, plus extra for dusting

For the white sauce

2 cups (16 fl oz/500 ml) whole milk

4 tablespoons (2 oz/60 g) unsalted butter

¼ cup (1½ oz/45 g) all-purpose (plain) flour

½ teaspoon kosher salt

¼ lb (125 g) Parmigiano-Reggiano cheese

Kosher salt for cooking the gnocchi

1 tablespoon unsalted butter

1 tablespoon plain fine dried bread crumbs

MAKES 6–8 SERVINGS

4 ›

5 ››

4 Adjust the dough consistency and divide the dough

Sprinkle ¼ cup (1½ oz/45 g) of the remaining flour on a wood or slightly rough plastic work surface. Spread the potato mixture on the surface and sprinkle with another ¼ cup of flour. Using the bench scraper and then your hands, scoop, lift, and fold the mixture, lightly pressing it as you work, until the flour is incorporated. Work in only as much of the final ½ cup (2½ oz/75 g) flour as needed for a smooth dough. Shape the dough into a ball, dust with flour, and cover with an overturned bowl. Dust 2 large rimmed baking sheets with flour. Using the bench scraper, scrape the work surface clean and then dust it with flour. Cut the dough into 8 equal pieces. Slip 7 of the pieces back under the bowl.

5 Roll the dough into a log

Place 1 dough piece in the center of the surface and shape it into a short cylinder. Using the fingers of both hands, roll the dough back and forth over the surface, gradually shifting your hands to the ends, to elongate it slowly into a narrow log about ½ inch (12 mm) in diameter.

6 Cut the log into pieces

Use a bench scraper or knife to cut the log into ¾-inch (2-cm) pillow-shaped pieces. Place the pieces in a single layer, not touching, on the baking sheets. Roll and cut the remaining dough pieces in the same way. Cover the baking sheets with aluminum foil and refrigerate for at least 1 hour or for up to overnight.

7 Make the white sauce

If you need help making white sauce, turn to page 28. In a small saucepan over medium heat, warm the milk. Place a nonreactive saucepan over medium-low heat and add the butter. When the butter has melted, add the flour and cook, stirring constantly, until the mixture forms a roux, 2–3 minutes. Remove from the heat and slowly add the hot milk while whisking constantly. Add the salt, return to medium heat, and cook, stirring constantly, until the sauce is smooth and thick enough to coat the back of a spoon, about 1 minute. Remove from the heat.

CHEF'S TIP
Don't try to make these dumplings with another potato variety. They will not have the proper starch and moisture content and thus will lack the correct texture.

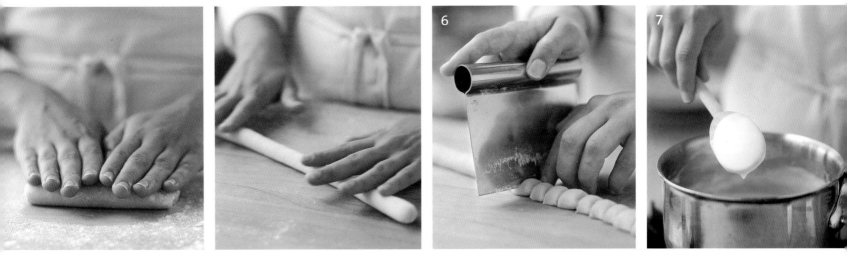

8 Ready your ingredients and equipment

Finely grate the cheese using the small grating holes of a box grater-shredder or a rasp grater. Set the cheese aside. Place a rack in the middle of the oven and preheat the oven to 400°F (200°C). Butter a 9-by-13-by-2-inch (23-by-33-by-5-inch) baking dish. Bring a large pot three-fourths full of water to a rolling boil and add about 2 tablespoons salt. Have ready a colander set over a bowl or in the sink.

MAKE-AHEAD TIP

This dish can be assembled and then refrigerated, covered tightly, for up to 24 hours before baking. You may need to add as much as 15 minutes to the cooking time. After it has baked for about 30 minutes, start checking it every 5 minutes to see if it is ready.

9 Cook the gnocchi

A few at a time, drop half of the gnocchi into the boiling water and stir them gently to prevent sticking. Let the gnocchi cook until they rise to the surface. This should take only about 3 minutes. To test the gnocchi for doneness, use a slotted spoon to remove one and use a paring knife to cut it in half. Bite into it; it should be tender throughout with no raw flour flavor. Using the slotted spoon, scoop out the gnocchi and place them in the colander to drain for a few seconds. Return the water to a rolling boil, add the remaining gnocchi, and cook and drain them as you did the first half.

10 Assemble the gratin

While the second batch of gnocchi is cooking, transfer the first batch to the prepared baking dish. Top the gnocchi with half of the white sauce and then half the cheese. Top with the second batch of drained gnocchi, pour on the remaining sauce, and sprinkle with the remaining cheese. Cut the butter into small bits and dot them over the sauce. Sprinkle evenly with the bread crumbs.

11 Bake and serve the gratin

Bake the gratin until the sauce is bubbling around the edges, the top is golden brown, and a knife inserted in the center comes out hot to the touch, about 30 minutes. Remove the dish from the oven, place on a wire rack, and let rest for about 10 minutes. Scoop out portions of the gnocchi with a large metal spoon, making sure each serving gets some of the golden brown top.

Serving ideas

Gnocchi are versatile, and baking them in a gratin is only one of many ways Italian cooks prepare them. Their light texture and delicate flavor pair well with many traditional pasta sauces. Here are three of my favorite choices: amatriciana sauce, pesto, and melted butter and cheese with freshly ground pepper. When tossing, gently layer the first batch of cooked gnocchi with half of the sauce, toss, and repeat to complete the dish.

Gnocchi with *amatriciana* sauce (top left)
Combining subtle gnocchi with robust Amatriciana Sauce (page 95), distinguished by hints of fiery chile and rich pancetta, yields a winning contrast.

Gnocchi with butter and Parmesan (left)
Toss the cooked gnocchi with ½ cup (4 oz/125 g) melted unsalted butter and ½ cup (2 oz/60 g) freshly grated Parmigiano-Reggiano cheese. Pass extra cheese and freshly ground pepper at the table.

Gnocchi with pesto (above)
Pesto (page 101) originated in Liguria, in northwestern Italy. There, cooks toss it with *trenette* (the local ribbon pasta), potatoes, and green beans, making it a natural partner for the potato gnocchi here.

Soba Noodles with Dipping Sauce

Japanese soba noodles boast a pleasing gray-brown color and an earthy flavor. Here, they are served cold, for dipping into a sauce that carries the subtle flavor of the sea from the addition of bonito flakes and *kombu*, a type of kelp. Use Japanese buckwheat flour, made from polished buckwheat, for the best results.

1 Make the dashi for the dipping sauce
In a saucepan over medium-low heat, combine the water and *kombu* and slowly heat until very hot but not simmering. Add the bonito flakes and remove the pan from the heat. The *kombu* and bonito flakes give off a strong smell or flavor if allowed to simmer or boil, so do not stray far from the stove. Let the broth stand until the flakes settle to the bottom of the pan, about 3 minutes. Pour the broth through a fine-mesh sieve into a clean saucepan and discard the *kombu* and bonito flakes. This simple, clear Japanese broth is known as *dashi*.

2 Make the dipping sauce
Place the saucepan with the dashi over medium heat, add the soy sauce, mirin, and sugar and cook, stirring once or twice, just until the sugar dissolves and steam rises from the pan, about 4 minutes. Remove the pan from the heat and let cool to room temperature.

3 Adjust the seasonings in the dipping sauce
Taste and evaluate the seasonings: If the sauce tastes flat, add a dash of soy sauce. If it tastes dull, add a touch more mirin. If it tastes harsh, smooth it out with a bit of sugar. Mix each seasoning in a little at a time until you achieve a flavor you like. Cover and refrigerate for about 2 hours to chill well.

4 Make the soba dough
Pour the ½ cup water into a small bowl, add the salt, and stir with a small whisk to dissolve. Put the buckwheat and all-purpose flours into a food processor fitted with the metal blade and pulse briefly to combine the flours. Turn on the machine and then gradually add the water mixture through the feed tube. Let the processor run just until the mixture forms a ball of dough on top of the blade, about 30 seconds. Gradually add the remaining 1–2 tablespoons water, a little bit at a time, if necessary just until the mixture comes together into a ball.

5 Lightly knead the dough by hand
Dust a wood or slightly rough plastic work surface and your hands with all-purpose flour and put the ball of dough in the center of the work surface. Use the heel of one hand to push the dough away from you, then lift and rotate it a quarter turn. Repeat the motion, dusting the dough lightly with all-purpose flour if necessary, until it feels damp but not sticky and is satiny. This will take only a minute or two. Shape the dough into a ball, cover it with a large overturned bowl, and let it rest for 30 minutes. ›

For the dipping sauce

4 cups (32 fl oz/1 l) water

1 piece *kombu*, 3 by 4 inches (7.5 by 10 cm)

½ cup dried bonito flakes

½ cup (4 fl oz/125 ml) Japanese soy sauce

⅓ cup (3 fl oz/80 ml) mirin

1 teaspoon sugar

For the soba dough

½ cup (4 fl oz/125 ml) water, plus 1–2 tablespoons water to adjust the consistency of the dough

2 teaspoons kosher salt

1¼ cups (6 oz/185 g) Japanese buckwheat flour

¾ cup (4 oz/125 g) unbleached all-purpose (plain) flour, plus extra for dusting

1 sheet nori, about 8 inches (20 cm) square

2 tablespoons wasabi powder

1–2 tablespoons water

8 green (spring) onions

1-inch (2.5-cm) knob fresh ginger

MAKES 6 SERVINGS

SHORTCUT
If you don't have time to make fresh soba, you can use 1 lb (500 g) dried soba. Cook the noodles in boiling water according to the instructions on the package and skip steps 4–9.

While the soba noodles dry, you'll have plenty of time to prepare the nori, green onions, wasabi, and ginger used to garnish and season the dish.

6 Knead the dough with a pasta machine

For help with kneading and rolling out fresh soba dough, turn to page 32. Secure the pasta machine onto your work surface and attach the crank. Lightly flour a rimmed baking sheet with all-purpose flour and set it nearby. Using a bench scraper or chef's knife, cut the dough into 4 equal pieces, then slip 3 of the pieces back under the bowl to keep the surface from drying out. Flatten 1 dough piece into a disk about ½ inch (12 mm) thick. Turn the dial on the pasta machine to the widest setting and dust the rollers with all-purpose flour. Crank the disk through the rollers. Fold the dough into thirds, dust 1 side with flour, and roll it through again. Repeat 8–10 times until the dough is smooth and satiny.

7 Roll out the dough into a sheet

Continue passing the dough through the rollers, moving the dial 1 notch narrower after each pass and lightly flouring the dough if it seems sticky (you don't need to fold it at this stage), until it is about 1/16 inch (2 mm) thick, usually after rolling on the second-to-last setting.

8 Cut the sheet into sections

Cut the soba sheets into sections about 10 inches (25 cm) long. Lay the sections flat on the floured baking sheet, layering them as needed and separating the layers with floured lint-free kitchen towels. Repeat steps 6–8 with the remaining dough pieces. Let dry for 10–20 minutes. (The drying will firm up the dough and make it easier to cut.)

9 Cut the sections into noodles

For more details on cutting fresh soba noodles, turn to page 33. Secure the linguine-cutting attachment (for the narrowest noodles) onto the pasta machine and attach the crank. One at a time, insert a section of dough into the blades and turn the crank to pass it through, creating strands about 1/16 inch (2 mm) wide. Spread the soba noodles out on a lightly floured rimmed baking sheet and let dry for 10–20 minutes while you prepare the nori, wasabi, green onions, and ginger.

10 Prepare the nori

Turn one of the burners on your stove to medium heat. Grasp the sheet of nori with tongs and pass it over the gas or the electric burner, keeping it about 3 inches (7.5 cm) above the heat. It will turn bright green and become crisp. Do not hold it over the heat too long, or it might catch fire. Place the toasted sheet of nori on a plate and let cool. Using kitchen shears, cut the cooled nori into quarters. Stack the pieces and cut the stack into strips ⅛ inch (3 mm) wide. Cut these strips in half crosswise. Set the nori strips aside.

11 Prepare the wasabi

In a small bowl, use a spoon to stir together the wasabi powder with 1 tablespoon of the water to form a thick paste. You may need to add a little more water if the paste is too thick. It should be soft and pliable.

12 Prepare the remaining accompaniments

Using the chef's knife, trim away the root ends and tough green tops of the green onions, and then thinly slice the onions crosswise. You should have about ½ cup (1½ oz/45 g) sliced green onions. Using a vegetable peeler or paring knife, peel away the thin brown skin from the ginger, then grate the ginger using an Asian ginger grater or a rasp grater.

13 Cook the noodles

Bring a large pot three-fourths full of water to a rolling boil. Do not add salt to the water as you would with Italian pasta; Japanese cooks do not salt the water when cooking noodles. Add the noodles all at once and stir them gently to prevent sticking. Let the noodles cook, stirring occasionally, until they are tender but still slightly chewy when you bite into them. This should take only about 2 minutes.

14 Drain the noodles

Pour the noodles in a colander to drain (be sure to use a colander with fine holes, so the thin noodles don't fall through). Rinse the noodles under running cool water until they are cold, carefully lifting and separating them with your fingers, then drain again. Soba noodles are more starchy than Italian pasta; you need to rinse them to remove the excess starch or they will stick together.

15 Serve the dish

Use your fingers to untangle the noodles gently, then arrange them in neat piles on 6 individual plates. Sprinkle each portion of noodles with an equal amount of the nori and green onions. Divide the chilled dipping sauce among 6 bowls, then divide the wasabi and ginger among 6 small saucers. Serve each diner a plate of noodles, a bowl of dipping sauce, and a saucer of wasabi and ginger. Provide both chopsticks and spoons. Instruct diners to season their dipping sauce with wasabi and ginger to taste, and then, using the chopsticks, dip the noodles into the sauce before eating. They will use the spoons to help lift the noodles to their mouths.

CHEF'S TIP

Troll ethnic markets for unfamiliar ingredients, especially when you are preparing an authentic recipe. I shop for the buckwheat flour, kombu, bonito flakes, nori, and wasabi for this recipe at a Japanese market near where I live.

Serving ideas

Cold soba noodles accompanied with a dashi-based dipping sauce is a popular dish in Japan. But soba noodles served in hot dashi are also common. Make the dashi and season it as directed for the dipping sauce, but instead of chilling it, bring it just to a simmer over medium heat. Use warm water when rinsing the noodles, then simply ladle the hot broth over the them. Garnish with the item of your choice (see below).

Soba in broth with green onions (top left)
Instead of chopping the green onions, try slivering them. Cut 4 green onions into 2-inch (5-cm) lengths and then slice lengthwise as thinly as possible. Scatter over the noodles.

Soba in broth with daikon (left)
Use a vegetable peeler to remove the outer layer of a daikon. Continue to peel off layers of white daikon underneath, then stack them and thinly slice. Scatter over the noodles and top with daikon sprouts.

Soba in broth with *shichimi* (above)
Shichimi is a typical Japanese condiment made of ground red chile, black pepper, sesame seeds, and other seasonings. It adds a bit of spice to this dish.

Pot Stickers

Like Italian pasta, pot sticker or wonton skins are made from wheat flour and water. Here, the wrappers enclose a traditional Chinese mixture of ground pork, napa cabbage, green onions, and spicy-sweet ginger. Panfried and then steamed, pot stickers develop a crisp, brown crust on the bottom and a soft, plump top.

1 Prepare and blanch the cabbage

Using a chef's knife, cut away the hard inner core from the cabbage, then cut the leaves crosswise into strips about ½ inch (12 mm) wide. Measure out 2 cups (6 oz/185 g) and reserve any remaining leaves for another use. Bring a saucepan three-fourths full of water to a rolling boil. Add the salt and cabbage, allow the water to return to a boil, and cook for 1 minute. The cabbage should be just wilted. (Chefs call this method for partially cooking a vegetable *blanching*.) Pour the cabbage into a colander to drain and rinse under running cold water until the cabbage is completely cool. Shake the colander well, then squeeze the cabbage with your hands to remove as much moisture as possible. The volume will be reduced to less than 1 cup.

2 Prepare the green onions and ginger

Using the chef's knife, trim away the root ends and tough green tops of the green onions, and then chop the onions finely. Using a vegetable peeler or paring knife, peel away the thin brown skin from the ginger, then grate the ginger using an Asian ginger grater or a rasp grater. Measure out 1 tablespoon ginger for the filling; set the remaining ginger aside.

3 Mix the filling

Place the cabbage in a food processor fitted with the metal blade and pulse until the cabbage is finely chopped. Add the green onions, the 1 tablespoon ginger, the pork, the soy sauce, and the cornstarch. Pulse just until the ingredients are evenly combined and the mixture holds together but still has some texture. Do not pulse too much, or the mixture will become pasty.

4 Adjust the seasonings

To check the seasonings, fry a small nugget of the filling mixture. Heat the peanut oil in a small frying pan over medium-high heat until the oil appears to shimmer. Place a small spoonful of the filling in the pan and cook until browned on both sides, about 3 minutes. Using tongs, remove the nugget from the pan and transfer to a plate. Let the nugget cool slightly, then taste it and evaluate the seasonings. If you feel the filling tastes a little flat, mix a drop or two of soy sauce or a small amount of salt into the remaining filling mixture. If you feel the flavor lacks zip, mix in a bit more green onion or ginger.

For the filling

½ head napa cabbage

1 teaspoon kosher salt

2 green (spring) onions

2–3-inch (5–7.5-cm) knob fresh ginger

½ lb (250 g) ground (minced) pork

2 tablespoons soy sauce

2 teaspoons cornstarch (cornflour)

1 tablespoon peanut oil or canola oil for frying the filling "nugget"

For the dipping sauce

½ cup (4 fl oz/125 ml) soy sauce

2 tablespoons seasoned rice vinegar

1 teaspoon Asian sesame oil

1 tablespoon peeled and grated fresh ginger

36 round pot sticker or wonton skins, each 2½ inches (6 cm) in diameter

1 egg white, lightly beaten

4 tablespoons (2 fl oz/60 ml) peanut oil or canola oil

½ cup (4 fl oz/125 ml) water

MAKES 36 POT STICKERS, OR 6 SERVINGS

CHEF'S TIP

If you can't find round pot sticker skins, buy large egg roll wrappers. Use a 2½-inch (6-cm) round pastry cutter to cut out circles of dough.

5 Make the dipping sauce
In a small bowl, combine the soy sauce, vinegar, sesame oil, and 1 tablespoon of the ginger you grated earlier and stir with a fork to mix well. Set the sauce aside to let the flavors marry.

6 Form the pot stickers
Line a large baking sheet with plastic wrap. Arrange 6 of the pot sticker skins on a work surface (keep the remaining skins in the package to prevent them from drying out). Using a pastry brush, very lightly brush one-half of the edge of each round with the egg white. They should be barely moist. Place 1 teaspoon of the filling mixture in the center of each skin. (Resist the urge to add more filling; the pot stickers will be too hard to pleat, and the mixture might leak out during cooking.) Fold the coated edge of the skin over the filling to meet the uncoated edge. Holding this half-moon in one hand, and using your thumb and index finger, pinch together the edges at one end of the curve. Then slowly work your way along the curve to the opposite end, making 4 or 5 evenly spaced, firmly sealed pleats over the length of the arc to enclose the filling completely. Finally, flatten the bottom slightly by pressing it gently against your palm. Place the pot sticker on the prepared baking sheet. Repeat the folding and pleating with the remaining skins and filling.

7 Fry the pot stickers
Preheat the oven to 200°F (95°C) and place a large platter in the oven to warm. Put a 12-inch (30-cm) nonstick frying pan over medium-high heat and add 2 tablespoons of the peanut oil. Warm the oil until a drop of water flicked into the pan sizzles immediately on contact. Carefully add about half of the pot stickers so they fit in a single layer without touching. Fry the pot stickers until they are golden on the bottom, 1–2 minutes. Watch them closely, as they brown quickly.

8 Steam the pot stickers
Carefully add ¼ cup (2 fl oz/60 ml) of the water to the pan. Stand back as you pour, as the water may spatter a bit when it comes in contact with the oil. Reduce the heat to low, cover the pan, and steam the pot stickers until the skins are slightly translucent, 2–3 minutes. Uncover and raise the heat to medium. Cook until the liquid in the pan has evaporated and the tops of the pot stickers have begun to puff up, about 1 minute. Using a slotted spatula, transfer the pot stickers to the warmed platter and cover them lightly with aluminum foil to keep warm. Repeat the frying and steaming steps with the rest of the pot stickers, adding the remaining 2 tablespoons peanut oil to the pan to fry the pot stickers and then steaming them in the remaining ¼ cup water.

9 Serve the pot stickers
Pour the dipping sauce into small dishes. Serve the pot stickers right away, with the dipping sauce alongside.

Pot Sticker Variations

Once you've mastered filling, folding, and pleating the classic Chinese pot stickers on page 123, you will want to try different fillings. Making the filling is the easiest part of any pot sticker recipe, usually requiring no more than a little chopping followed by a brief whirl in a food processor. The variations below offer a trio of appealing options, including two vegetarian fillings, one of mixed vegetables and one of mushrooms and green onion, and an elegant version that calls for crabmeat. You could also make some of each; all three are enhanced by the ginger-spiked soy dipping sauce. Serve these as a first course or a snack. Each variation makes 6 servings.

Vegetable Pot Stickers

Carrots and shiitake mushrooms stand in for the ground pork in this delicious filling, appreciated by vegetarians and non-vegetarians alike.

Follow the recipe for Pot Stickers, replacing the filling with the one that follows.

To make the vegetable filling, bring a saucepan three-fourths full of water to a rolling boil. Add 1 teaspoon kosher salt, 4 cups (12 oz/375 g) sliced napa cabbage, 6 fresh shiitake mushroom caps, and 1 cup (4 oz/125 g) shredded carrot. Allow the water to return to a boil, cook the vegetables for 1 minute, then pour into a colander to drain. Squeeze the vegetables to remove as much moisture as possible.

Add the blanched vegetables to a food processor and pulse to chop finely. Add 2 chopped green (spring) onions, white and tender green parts; 1 tablespoon peeled and grated fresh ginger; 2 tablespoons soy sauce; and 2 teaspoons cornstarch (cornflour). Pulse just until the ingredients are evenly combined and the mixture holds together but still has some texture. Adjust the seasonings.

Mushroom Pot Stickers

In this filling, mushrooms and green onions with a hint of garlic replace the pork and cabbage.

Follow the recipe for Pot Stickers, replacing the filling with the one that follows.

To make the mushroom filling, in a frying pan over medium heat, warm 2 tablespoons peanut or canola oil. Add ¼ cup (¾ oz/20 g) chopped green (spring) onions, white and tender green parts, and 1 teaspoon chopped garlic. Cook until fragrant, about 1 minute. Stir in 6 oz (185 g) sliced fresh shiitake or button mushrooms and sauté until any liquid evaporates and the mushrooms are tender, about 10 minutes. Let the mixture cool slightly.

Scrape the mixture into a food processor and pulse to chop finely. Transfer to a bowl, stir in 2 tablespoons soy sauce, and then stir in 1 teaspoon cornstarch (cornflour). If the mixture is too moist to hold its shape, stir in an additional 1 teaspoon cornstarch. Adjust the seasonings.

Crab Pot Stickers

Here, crabmeat replaces the ground pork, creating a unique seafood pot sticker.

Follow the recipe for Pot Stickers, replacing the filling with the one that follows.

To make the crab filling, prepare and blanch ½ head napa cabbage. Squeeze the cabbage to remove as much moisture as possible.

Put the blanched cabbage in a food processor and pulse to chop finely. Add 2 chopped green (spring) onions, white and tender green parts; 1 tablespoon peeled and grated fresh ginger; ½ lb (250 g) finely chopped fresh-cooked crabmeat, picked over for any shell fragments or cartilage; 2 tablespoons soy sauce; and 2 teaspoons cornstarch (cornflour). Pulse just until the ingredients are evenly combined and the mixture holds together but still has some texture. (Do not pulse too much, or the mixture will become pasty.) Adjust the seasonings.

Pad Thai

These Thai-inspired noodles are a symphony of flavors and textures: sweetness from the sugar, saltiness from the fish sauce, tartness from the lime juice, fire from the chile, crunch from the peanuts and bean sprouts, and softness from the rice noodles, eggs, and shrimp. A crown of garnishes, including fresh cilantro and basil, adds yet another layer of color and flavor.

1 package (7 oz/220 g) dried flat rice noodles, ¼ inch (6 mm) wide

For the sauce

¼ cup (2 fl oz/60 ml) Asian fish sauce

2 tablespoons fresh lime or lemon juice

2 tablespoons sugar

2 tablespoons peanut oil or canola oil

½ lb (250 g) shrimp (prawns), peeled and deveined (page 139)

3 cloves garlic, minced (page 45)

¼ teaspoon red pepper flakes

3 large eggs, lightly beaten

2 cups (4 oz/120 g) bean sprouts

4 tablespoons (1 oz/30 g) coarsely chopped unsalted roasted peanuts

4 tablespoons (1½ oz/45 g) thinly sliced green (spring) onions, white and tender green parts

½ cup (¾ oz/20 g) chopped fresh cilantro (fresh coriander) (page 39)

¼ cup (⅓ oz/10 g) chiffonade of fresh basil or mint (page 39)

MAKES 4 SERVINGS

1 Soak the noodles
Bring a saucepan three-fourths full of water to a rolling boil. Remove the saucepan from the heat (you don't want to cook the noodles in boiling water over the heat or they will become too soft). Drop the noodles into the water and stir well. Let the noodles stand until tender, about 30 minutes. Pour the noodles into a large colander to drain.

2 Make the sauce
In a small bowl, combine the fish sauce, lime juice, and sugar and stir with a fork to dissolve the sugar. Set the sauce aside, but keep it near the stove.

3 Stir-fry the ingredients
Preheat the oven to 200°F (95°C) and place a large platter in the oven to warm. Place a large frying pan or wok over medium-high heat. When hot, add the oil and heat until it appears to shimmer. Add the shrimp, garlic, and red pepper flakes and, using a flat-bottomed wooden spoon or wooden spatula, stir and toss until fragrant, about 1 minute. Pour in the eggs and let them cook, without stirring, until lightly set, about 30 seconds. Then, stir well to scramble the eggs with the shrimp. Add the fish sauce mixture and drained noodles and cook, lifting and stirring the noodles constantly, until the ingredients are well blended, about 2 minutes. Stir in 1 cup (2 oz/60 g) of the the bean sprouts, 2 tablespoons of the nuts, and 2 tablespoons of the green onions, and cook, stirring, until heated through and evenly distributed, about 1 minute longer. (The remaining bean sprouts, nuts, and green onions will be sprinkled on top as a garnish just before serving.)

4 Adjust the seasonings
Taste the mixture and evaluate the seasonings: If the mixture tastes dull, add a bit more fish sauce or lime juice. If you think it needs more spice, add more red pepper flakes. Mix each seasoning in a little at a time until you achieve a flavor you like.

5 Garnish and serve the dish
Using a large spoon and spatula, transfer the noodles to the warmed platter. Garnish with the cilantro, basil, and the remaining bean sprouts, peanuts, and green onions. Serve right away.

Vietnamese Rice Noodles with Grilled Chicken

Named after their resemblance to the Italian noodles called "vermicelli," these ultrathin rice noodles serve as a neutral base for raw vegetables and herbs. The sauce, a tasty blend of ingredients popular in Southeast Asia, brightens both the noodle-vegetable salad and the hot grilled chicken that tops it.

1 Make the sauce

In a small bowl, stir together the ginger, 1–2 teaspoons of the chile (depending on how spicy you like your food), the garlic, vinegar, lemon juice, fish sauce, and sugar until the sugar dissolves. Taste the sauce; it should be a nice mixture of spicy, sour, salty, and sweet. If you feel the flavor is out of balance, add any of the ingredients a little at a time until you achieve a flavor that you like.

2 Marinate the chicken

Place the chicken breasts in a nonreactive bowl and spoon 2 tablespoons of the sauce over it. Turn the chicken to coat evenly with the sauce, cover, and refrigerate until ready to cook.

3 Prepare the remaining ingredients

Bring a saucepan three-fourths full of water to a rolling boil. Remove the saucepan from the heat (you don't want to cook the noodles in boiling water over the heat or they will become too soft). With your hands, break up the rice noodles into 4-inch (10-cm) pieces. Drop the noodles into the water and stir well. Let the noodles stand until tender, about 30 minutes. Pour the noodles into a large colander to drain. In a large bowl, combine the bean sprouts, carrot, cucumber, green onions, mint, and cilantro. Stir and toss to combine.

4 Cook the chicken

Place a ridged grill pan over medium-high heat. When the pan is hot, use a brush to coat the surface evenly with the oil. Place the chicken on the grill pan and cook until nicely browned on the first side, 3–4 minutes. Turn the chicken over and continue to cook until nicely browned on the second side and no longer pink when cut into with a knife, 3–4 minutes longer. Transfer the chicken to a cutting board and, using a sharp knife, cut on the diagonal into slices ¼ inch (6 mm) thick. Cover the slices with aluminum foil to keep warm.

5 Assemble and serve the dish

Add the noodles to the bowl holding the vegetables and herbs and toss well. Add all but about 2 tablespoons of the remaining sauce and toss again to coat evenly. Divide the noodle mixture evenly among 4 individual plates. Arrange the hot chicken slices on top of the noodles and vegetables, dividing them evenly. Drizzle the remaining sauce over the chicken and serve right away.

For the sauce

2 tablespoons peeled and grated fresh ginger

1–2 teaspoons chopped serrano chile

1 teaspoon finely minced garlic (page 45)

⅓ cup (3 fl oz/80 ml) seasoned rice vinegar

3 tablespoons fresh lemon juice

3 tablespoons Asian fish sauce

1 tablespoon sugar

2 whole boneless, skinless chicken breasts, about 1 lb (500 g) total weight

1 package (7 oz/220 g) dried rice vermicelli

3 cups (6 oz /185 g) bean sprouts

1 cup (3½ oz/105 g) shredded peeled carrot

1 cup (5 oz/155 g) unpeeled, thin half-moon English (hothouse) cucumber slices

¼ cup (1½ oz/45 g) chopped green (spring) onions, white and tender green parts

¼ cup (⅓ oz/10 g) chopped fresh mint (page 39)

¼ cup (⅓ oz/10 g) chopped fresh cilantro (fresh coriander) (page 39)

1 tablespoon peanut oil or canola oil

MAKES 4 SERVINGS

CHEF'S TIP
Don't be alarmed by the aroma of fish sauce. While it may be off-putting when sampled directly from the bottle, it adds unmatched depth and authentic flavor to Vietnamese- and Thai-inspired dishes.

Chinese Noodles with Pork & Spicy Peanut Sauce

A staple in many parts of China, wheat noodles are often paired with meat and a bold brown sauce to make a hearty snack or meal. This easy version features ground pork and a balanced blend of sweet hoisin sauce, smooth peanut butter, salty soy sauce, and a touch of fiery chile. Minced green onions add a nice color contrast.

For the sauce

1 cup (8 fl oz/250 ml) canned low-sodium chicken broth

¼ cup (2 fl oz/60 ml) hoisin sauce

2 tablespoons soy sauce

1 tablespoon peanut oil or canola oil

¾ lb (375 g) ground (minced) pork

Pinch of red pepper flakes

1 cup (3 oz/90 g) minced green (spring) onions, white and tender green parts, plus a little extra for serving, if desired

1 tablespoon minced garlic (page 45)

1 tablespoon peeled and grated fresh ginger

2 tablespoons creamy peanut butter

1 lb (500 g) thin fresh Chinese egg noodles

1 teaspoon hot chile oil

MAKES 4 MAIN-COURSE SERVINGS OR 6 FIRST-COURSE SERVINGS

1 **Make the sauce**
In a small bowl, stir together the broth, hoisin sauce, and soy sauce; set aside. Place a 12-inch (30-cm) frying pan over medium heat and add the peanut oil. When the oil appears to shimmer, add the ground pork and red pepper flakes and cook, stirring frequently, until the meat is crumbly and the color changes from pink to gray, about 10 minutes. Add ½ cup (1½ oz/45 g) of the green onions, the garlic, and ginger to the pan and mix well with the pork. Add the broth mixture and peanut butter, stir well, and cook until small bubbles form on the surface. Cook until the peanut butter is melted and the sauce is slightly thickened, about 5 minutes. Remove the sauce from the heat.

2 **Adjust the seasonings**
Taste the sauce. If you feel it tastes dull, add more hoisin sauce or soy sauce. If you think it needs more spice, add more red pepper flakes or ginger. Mix each seasoning in a little at a time until you achieve a flavor you like, keeping in mind that the sauce will mellow once it is mixed with the noodles.

3 **Cook and drain the noodles**
Preheat the oven to 200°F (95°C) and place individual plates in the oven to warm. Bring a large pot three-fourths full of water to a rolling boil. Do not add salt to the water; Chinese cooks do not salt the water when cooking noodles. Add the noodles all at once, stir gently, and cook until the noodles are tender, but still slightly chewy. This should take only 2–3 minutes. While the noodles are cooking, reheat the sauce in the pan over medium-low heat. Pour the noodles into a colander to drain, then shake the colander to remove the excess water. Don't let the strands get too dry, or they will stick together.

4 **Toss the noodles with the sauce**
Add the drained noodles to the pan with the sauce. Using 2 wooden spoons or spatulas, toss the noodles until they are evenly coated with the sauce and the pork is evenly distributed. Add the remaining ½ cup green onions and the chile oil and toss to distribute evenly.

5 **Serve the dish**
Using the spoons or spatulas, divide the noodle mixture evenly among the warmed plates. Garnish with minced green onions, if desired. Serve right away.

Flour start 100

Plate Tare   350 g

Bowl Tare   313   start egg   57g
                                     53
                                     4

Potato   128 g
Flour   ~~35 g~~ 65g
Egg   44g   384   326
                     300   313
                      3   13

Gnocchi Proportions Prelim
   per 100g Potato /Riced
       51g   All purpose Flour
       35g   Beaten Egg

Proud supporter of World Wildlife Fund

Using Key Tools & Equipment

Anyone who has ever stepped into an unfamiliar kitchen and improvised meal preparations with a few battered pots, pans, and knives knows that carefully selected cookware is the difference between something to eat and a memorable meal. Before you try your hand at preparing pasta, check the contents of your cupboards. Even such basics as a suitably sized pan and a reliably sharp knife can determine the success of what you cook.

Tools for Making Pasta

Mixing pasta dough can be easy with the assistance of a few pieces of essential kitchen equipment. First, a food processor eases the work of mixing the dough. Just combine the ingredients in the work bowl fitted with the metal blade and turn on the machine. A food processor is also handy for making bread crumbs for meatballs and for chopping the fillings for ravioli and pot stickers.

After you mix the dough, you'll need a large work surface on which you can knead the dough briefly. The ideal surface is wood, which will grip and hold the flour used for dusting. A butcher-block countertop or a heavy cutting board is a good choice. A rough plastic surface can be substituted, but marble is too slippery. After you've kneaded the dough, you can easily divide it into workable quantities with a straight-edged bench scraper.

The second machine you'll need is a pasta machine, which simplifies kneading, rolling, and cutting pasta. The machine consists of two main parts. The larger part houses a set of rollers. You narrow the width between the rollers by adjusting the wheel on the side and feed the pasta through the rollers by inserting the crank on the opposite side. Secure this part to a countertop with the clamp provided and run a small piece of dough through the widest setting 8 to 10 times to knead it. Adjust the rollers to narrow the the space between them and progressively run the pasta through to make a thin sheet.

Use the second part of the machine to cut the pasta sheets into strands. Most machines come with a cutting attachment with two rows of teeth, one for cutting narrow strands, such as linguine, and one

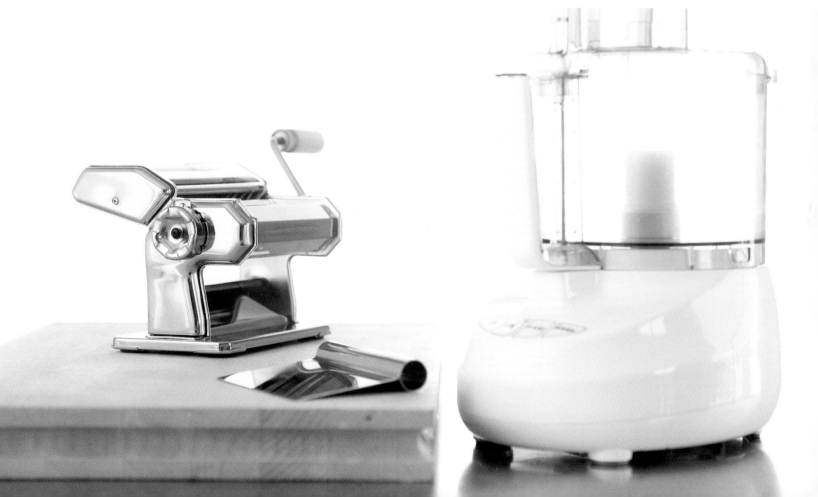

for cutting wider strips, such as fettuccine. You can purchase separate attachments for cutting fresh angel hair and spaghetti.

Measuring Tools

Ensure accuracy in your cooking with dependable measuring tools. Begin with liquid measuring cups: 1-cup (8–fl oz/ 250-ml) and 4-cup (1-l) sizes are imperative, and a 2-cup (16–fl oz/500-ml) size is handy as well. For flour and other dry ingredients, invest in a nested set of dry measuring cups. For small quantities of spices, herbs, salt, and oils, you'll need a set of measuring spoons.

Graters & Grinders

Tools for grating and grinding foods grow more sophisticated all the time. A multisided stainless-steel box grater-shredder can be used to grate, shred, or slice, depending on the side you use.

Innovative rasp graters—choose different-sized rasps to achieve different effects—have become indispensable in many kitchens. You'll also find well-designed porcelain ginger graters, and metal nutmeg graters (not pictured) with a small compartment for stowing the spice. A pepper mill is needed for freshly ground pepper, and a mortar and a pestle will allow you to make pesto the time-honored way.

Basic Cutlery

Good knives are fundamental tools for every kind of cooking, including the making of pasta doughs and pasta sauces. A heavy chef's knife is used for everything from chopping vegetables to mincing herbs to halving tomatoes. Select a sharp paring knife for miscellaneous cutting jobs and an efficient vegetable peeler for paring carrots and potatoes.

Filled Pasta Tools

You'll need a pastry brush to moisten the edges of filled pastas to seal them and a fluted pastry wheel to cut their scalloped edges. Use a plain-edged pizza cutter for cutting fresh pasta sheets into strips for lasagna, ravioli, or tortellini.

Mixing Bowls

You can never have too many mixing bowls. The smaller ones can hold prepped ingredients; the largest bowl can be inverted over pasta dough while it rests. Look for tempered glass bowls that can be used for hot mixtures, too.

Baking Sheets

An assortment of rimmed full-, half-, and quarter-sheet pans are handy for holding rolled-out pasta strips and finished pasta shapes. Be sure to dust them lightly with flour before adding the pasta.

Pasta-Cooking Pots & Colanders

You need a big pot for boiling pasta. A heavy 8-quart (8-l) stockpot made of stainless steel or brushed or anodized aluminum is a good choice. A two-handled model allows you to grasp it firmly with both hands when you drain the pasta. If you cook pasta often, consider a pot with its own lift-out pasta insert (sometimes called a pasta pentola) for draining pasta quickly. Otherwise, have a large colander on hand.

Frying Pans

A frying pan 12 inches (30 cm) in diameter is ideal for making most sauces. It's big enough for tossing together the sauce and a pound (500 g) of pasta and can be made of the same material as your pasta pot. Flared sides facilitate stirring and lifting foods as they cook. A nonstick

cooking surface is recommended for panfrying and steaming pot stickers, and streamlines cleanup after cooking any sauce. Other useful pans include a large, straight-sided sauté pan for Bolognese Sauce (page 49) and a wok for stir-frying Asian noodles.

Saucepans

Saucepans are invaluable for pasta making, especially for cooking cream sauces. Useful sizes include a small (1- to 1½-qt/ 1- to 1.5-l) pan for warming milk and a medium (about 2-qt/2-l) pan for making White Sauce (page 28). To prevent cream sauces from discoloring and tomato and other acidic sauces from developing off flavors, choose pans lined with or made of a nonreactive material, such as stainless steel or porcelain enamel. Many serious cooks favor copper pans

because they conduct heat efficiently. If you invest in them, make sure they are lined with nonreactive stainless steel.

Baking Dishes

For making lasagna and other baked pastas, you'll need a heatproof 9-by-13-by-2-inch (23-by-33-by-5-cm) baking dish. It can be made of tempered glass, porcelain, earthenware, or enameled cast iron. A nonreactive interior prevents the discoloration of cream sauces or off flavors in tomato sauces. Round baking dishes that hold about 2 quarts (2 l) can be used as well.

Wooden Spoons & Spatulas

You'll need a selection of wooden spoons and spatulas for moving around sauce ingredients in pans so they mix together and cook without sticking to the bottom.

Use a sturdy, long-handled wooden spoon to stir sauces and a wooden spoon with a flat bottom or a spatula to get into the corners of frying pans when you deglaze meat sauces. Two large, same-sized wooden spoons or spatulas are perfect for tossing together pasta and sauce. Heatproof silicone spatulas, which can withstand temperatures up to 500°F (260°C), are good for high-heat cooking.

Metal Spoons & Serving Tools

Have a large metal spoon on hand for serving filled or baked pastas, and a sturdy spatula for lasagna. A claw-shaped pasta fork simplifies serving strand pastas such as spaghetti or fettuccine.

A large metal spoon makes quick work of skimming fat from cooked meats. A slotted metal spoon is perfect for lifting out filled pastas or blanched tomatoes from boiling water, while a ladle (not pictured) is handy for scooping out pasta-cooking water for thinning a sauce.

Heavy-duty metal tongs are used for lifting out a piece of cooked pasta to taste-test, for removing pasta strands from a colander, or for transferring a meatball or sausage from a pan or serving dish to a dinner plate.

Linens

Equip your kitchen with reliable pot holders, oven mitts, and heavy kitchen towels. They should be heavy enough to protect your hands from the heat of steaming liquids and hot ovens.

Measuring & Portioning Tools

Have a ruler on hand for measuring the length of pasta strips for ravioli, and for determining the length for fresh noodles such as fettuccine. A teaspoon from a traditional flatware set is great for portioning out filling amounts for filled pastas. And a 2-inch (5-cm) spring-action ice cream scoop makes scooping out the correct amount for meatballs easy.

Miscellaneous Equipment

These tools may not immediately come to mind for making pasta, but they are useful in any kitchen. A ricer makes quick work of processing baked potatoes for gnocchi. A flat sauce whisk efficiently mixes butter and flour for a roux. An instant-read thermometer gauges the temperature of warm water when making some pastas. Finally, lint-free kitchen towels are useful for wringing dry cooked spinach, for blotting cooked lasagna noodles, and, when dusted with flour, for separating sheets of rolled-out pasta.

Glossary

ANCHOVIES These tiny, silver-skinned fish appear widely in Italian cooking and are a traditional ingredient in Puttanesca Sauce (page 95). Anchovy fillets packed in olive oil are commonly available in tins, but look for higher-quality fillets sold in glass jars.

ARUGULA Also known as rocket, these slender, green, deeply notched leaves have an appealing mild peppery taste. Arugula is much favored in Italy, where it is often used in salads and pasta sauces.

BEAN SPROUTS These edible sprouts, also known as mung bean sprouts, have a refreshing, crunchy texture that is excellent in cold noodle dishes. About 2 inches (5 cm) long, the sprouts have yellow-green heads and silvery white stems. Refrigerate the highly perishable sprouts in an airtight container for no longer than 3 days.

BONITO FLAKES These delicate, buff-colored flakes, known as *katsuobushi*, are shaved from a bonito fish that has been dried and smoked. The shavings have a subtle fish taste and aroma and are one of the principal ingredients in bonito stock, or dashi (page 117). Keep the flakes in a sealed container in a cool, dry place.

BREAD CRUMBS Use plain fine dried bread crumbs to make crisp toppings for oven-baked pasta dishes or to lend body to fillings and meatballs. You can purchase bread crumbs, often sold in canisters, at most supermarkets, or you can make them yourself (see the Chef's Tip on page 87). If you buy them, be sure not to get seasoned crumbs, which contain salt, dried herbs, and cheese that can interfere with the other flavors in your recipe.

BROCCOLI RABE Also known as broccoli raab, rape, and rapini, broccoli rabe paired with orecchiette is a traditional Italian pasta dish (page 63). This bright green vegetable, with its stalks and small florets, resembles regular broccoli, but it has many more leaves, which are small with jagged edges. Broccoli rabe has a mild, pleasantly bitter taste. Before cooking it, be sure to remove and discard any tough stems and wilted leaves.

BROTH A commercially made, well-flavored liquid made from cooking chicken, meat, or vegetables in water. Cooks in Italy use simple homemade broths. Canned broths tend to be saltier than homemade, so seek out a major brand that offers "low-sodium" or "reduced-sodium" varieties so you can better control the flavors in your final dish.

BUTTER, UNSALTED Butter that is unsalted is preferable to salted because it allows the cook more control over the seasoning of a dish. In addition, unsalted butter tends to be fresher because salt acts as a preservative, lengthening the shelf life of butter at the supermarket. Refrigerate unsalted butter in its original wrapping for up to 6 weeks. European-style butter, made from fermented cream, contains more butterfat and less water than regular butter, giving it a pure, rich buttery flavor.

CABBAGE, NAPA This cabbage variety typically has a large, elongated head of tightly packed leaves with fleshy bases and crinkled, pale green tops. The mild flavor and crunchy texture of napa cabbage make it a good candidate for stuffing pot stickers. It is also called Chinese cabbage.

CAPERS The unopened flower buds of bushes native to the Mediterranean, capers are dried, cured, and then usually packed in a vinegar brine. They add a pleasant tang to recipes and are a traditional ingredient in Puttanesca Sauce (page 95).

CHEESES
Visiting a good cheese shop is a rewarding experience, since you can often sample a cheese before you buy it. When preparing cheese for pasta, be sure to freshly grate or shred it just before using. The freshness of flavor that this step adds will be noticeable in the final results.

Cheddar First made in the village of Cheddar in England, this cheese has a tangy, salty flavor, which ranges from mild to sharp, depending on age. Although naturally white, Cheddar is often dyed orange with annatto, a paste made from achiote seeds.

Fontina This cow's milk cheese has a mild flavor, slightly creamy texture, and a light but heady aroma. The Val d'Aosta, or Aosta Valley, of northwestern Italy produces the finest Fontina.

Goat When fresh, cheese made from goat's milk is mild, creamy, and slightly tangy. It becomes distinctly sharper in flavor as it ages. You can often find fresh, bright white goat cheese sold in disks or logs at well-stocked grocery stores.

Gorgonzola A cow's milk blue cheese from Italy with a moist, creamy texture and a complex, pleasantly pungent flavor.

Gruyère This semifirm, dense, smooth cow's milk cheese is produced in Switzerland and France and is appreciated for its mild, nutty flavor and superior melting properties.

Mascarpone A very soft, rich, smooth fresh Italian cheese made from cream, with a texture reminiscent of sour cream. Look for it packed in plastic tubs.

Mozzarella This mild, creamy cheese made from cow's milk or water buffalo's milk is formed into balls. If possible, seek out fresh mozzarella, which is sold surrounded by a little of the whey, rather than the larger, dry vacuum-sealed cheeses.

Parmigiano-Reggiano This firm, aged, salty cheese is made from partially skimmed cow's milk. It has a rich, nutty flavor and a pleasant granular texture that make it ideal for grating over pasta, adding to pesto, or mixing into fillings. Parmigiano-Reggiano is the most renowned of all Parmesan cheeses. It is produced in the Emilia-Romagna region of Italy, and its rind is always labeled with its trademarked name, Parmigiano-Reggiano.

Pecorino romano A pleasantly salty, Italian sheep's milk cheese with a grainy texture, *pecorino romano* is primarily used for grating. It has a sharp, pungent flavor and is traditionally called for in recipes that originate in the region surrounding Rome, where the cheese was first made.

Ricotta This fluffy, soft, mild cheese sold in plastic tubs is made by heating the whey left over from making pecorino and other cheeses. You can use part-skim or whole-milk varieties for the recipes in this book.

CLAMS, MANILA These small, sweet, hard-shelled clams are farmed off the Pacific Coast of the United States, although they are not native. Most are harvested when they are barely 1 inch (2.5 cm) in diameter. They are also known as Japanese clams.

CORNSTARCH Also called cornflour, cornstarch is a highly refined, silky powder ground from the endosperm of corn. It has nearly twice the thickening power of flour and is regularly used to absorb moisture in fillings for pot stickers and other dumplings.

CRABMEAT When a recipe calls for crabmeat, the easiest solution is to seek out fresh lump crabmeat sold at fish markets. It yields the sweetest, moistest meat. If unavailable, use good-quality frozen crabmeat that has been thawed, lightly rinsed, and well drained before chopping.

CREAM, HEAVY Also known as double cream and often labeled "heavy whipping cream," heavy cream usually contains from 36 to 40 percent fat. This high percentage of milk fat is what gives the cream its rich flavor. When used in a sauce, it can be boiled without separating. Look for cream that has been pasteurized but not ultrapasteurized for the best flavor.

DAIKON This common white-fleshed Asian radish has a sweet, mild taste and crunchy texture and is used extensively in Japanese cooking, often cut into threads or shredded for a garnish. Daikon is cylindrical and may grow up to 20 inches (50 cm) in length. Fresh daikon sprouts are also available and should be well rinsed before using.

EGGS Eggs are sometimes used partially cooked in sauces. All eggs have a small chance of being infected with salmonella or other bacteria, and not cooking them thoroughly can lead to food poisoning. This risk is of most concern to young children, elders, pregnant women, and anyone with a compromised immune system. If you have health and safety concerns, do not consume partially cooked eggs.

FISH SAUCE This amber liquid is the filtered extract of small fish, salt, and water left to ferment in the sun. The resulting sharp taste and acrid aroma mellow with cooking, and the sauce is a common seasoning used throughout Southeast Asia. Fish sauces vary in character. Thai fish sauce, called *nam pla,* tends to be paler and milder than Vietnamese fish sauce, known as *nuoc mam.*

FLOUR
One of the oldest and most important foods in the human diet, flour plays a major role in providing the body and substance in recipes for pasta and noodles. When we think of flour, we most often think of ground wheat grain, but it may be made from other ingredients as well.

All-purpose Two general types of wheat are grown: hard wheat, which is higher in gluten, and soft wheat, which has less gluten and more starch. All-purpose, or plain, flour is a mixture of the two flours and is well suited for making a wide range of foods, including pasta and noodles. This book recommends using unbleached flour, since it has a better flavor than bleached flour, which has been treated with chemicals.

Buckwheat Made by milling the seeds of an herb, this dark flour has a nutty, slightly sweet flavor and firm texture. When using it to make the soba noodles in this book, be sure to seek out buckwheat flour from Japan, where the seeds are polished to remove some of the dark hull before milling. This results in a particularly light, fine flour. Buckwheat flour is highly perishable, so store it in the refrigerator in an airtight container. Let it come to room temperature before using.

Semolina This flour is ground from a particular variety of wheat, called durum wheat, that is especially hard and high in gluten. It is used primarily for making dried pastas, and the best-quality brands include the promise of 100 percent durum semolina on the package. When using semolina flour for making fresh pasta, be sure to purchase finely, rather than coarsely, milled flour.

GINGER A refreshing combination of spicy and sweet in both aroma and flavor, ginger adds a lively note to many recipes, especially Asian dishes. Although often called a root, ginger is actually a rhizome, or underground stem. Select ginger that is firm and heavy, with smooth, unbroken skin.

HERBS
Using fresh herbs is one of the best things you can do to improve your cooking. Dried herbs do have their place, but fresh herbs usually bring brighter flavors to a dish. Store long-stemmed fresh herbs, such as basil or parsley, in the refrigerator with the ends submerged in a glass of water and a plastic bag placed over the top; the herbs should stay fresh for several days. Store dried herbs in airtight containers away from light and heat and replace them every 4 to 6 months, as they fade in color, fragrance, and flavor.

Basil Used in kitchens throughout the Mediterranean and in Southeast Asia, basil adds a highly aromatic, peppery flavor when used fresh.

Cilantro Also called fresh coriander and Chinese parsley, cilantro is a distinctly flavored herb used extensively in Mexican, Asian, Latin, and Middle Eastern cuisines. Cilantro's aniselike aroma and astringent taste are distinctive; use it sparingly at first until you are familiar with its flavor. When shopping, do not confuse cilantro and flat-leaf (Italian) parsley, which look similar.

Oregano This aromatic, pungent, and spicy herb is also known as wild marjoram. It is one of the few herbs that retains its flavor well even when dried, and it is an especially good match with tomatoes.

Parsley, flat-leaf This dark green Italian version of the faintly peppery herb adds vibrant color and pleasing flavor to many pasta sauces. It is far more flavorful than the curly-leaf type.

Thyme Tiny green leaves on thin stems, this herb is a mild, all-purpose seasoning with a floral, earthy flavor.

HOISIN SAUCE This spicy, slightly sweet, brownish red sauce is made from fermented soybeans enlivened with five-spice powder, garlic, and dried chile. It is widely available in bottles and jars in the Asian section of most supermarkets.

KOMBU A type of dried sea kelp, *kombu* is dark olive green and covered with a white salt residue. It has a strong "seafood" taste and fragrance and is most commonly used as a flavoring for Japanese dashi (page 117).

MIRIN An important ingredient in Japanese cuisine, mirin is a sweet cooking wine made by fermenting glutinous rice and sugar. The pale gold and syrupy wine adds a rich flavor when added to a dish or dipping sauce.

MUSHROOMS
Mushrooms, with their deep, earthy flavor, are an excellent addition to many pasta dishes. They are often ingredients in creamy sauces and are a common addition to fillings for pot stickers and ravioli or tortellini.

Oyster Cream to pale gray, oyster mushrooms have a fan shape and a subtle flavor of shellfish. They used to only grow wild but are now cultivated. Look for small, young mushrooms, as they become tough and bitter as they age.

White This variety is the cultivated all-purpose mushroom stocked in most markets. It is sometimes called a button mushroom, although the term refers specifically to the young, tender mushrooms with closed caps. For general cooking, use medium-sized mushrooms with few or no gills showing.

NONREACTIVE A term used to describe a pan or dish made of or lined with a material—stainless steel, enamel, ceramic, and glass—that will not react with acidic ingredients, such as tomatoes.

NOODLES
In this book, the term *noodles* is used for the vast array of Asian pasta varieties. Like Italian pasta, they may be made from wheat flour, but other flours are used as well, including rice and buckwheat.

Flat rice These semitransparent noodles are made from rice flour and are ⅛–¼ inch (3–6 mm) wide.

Fresh Chinese egg Varying from fine to thick, these pale yellow noodles are made from a dough of wheat flour, water, and eggs. Use noodles about ⅛ inch (3 mm) thick for the recipe in this book.

Rice vermicelli These brittle, creamy white noodles are extruded fine strands made from rice flour and water. They are sometimes called rice stick noodles.

Soba Typically made from a mixture of buckwheat and wheat flour, these Japanese noodles are grayish beige and are available both fresh or dried. They often have square-cut edges.

NORI A variety of marine alga, nori is dried and then compressed into paper-thin sheets that range in color from dark green to near black. It is often used as a garnish for soba noodles and is also a common wrapping for sushi. Toast nori before using to bring out its subtle flavor.

NUTMEG The seed of a tropical evergreen tree, a nutmeg has a hard shell and is about ¼ inch (2 cm) long. The slightly sweet spice should be bought whole and freshly grated on the fine rasps of a nutmeg or similar grater just before using. Nutmeg is often used to season creamy pasta sauces.

OIL
Oils play an essential role in the kitchen. A recipe's other ingredients and its heat requirements usually will suggest which oil is appropriate to use. As a general rule, choose less refined, more flavorful oils for uncooked uses such as drizzling and tossing, and refined, blander oils for cooking.

Asian sesame This deep amber-colored oil is pressed from toasted sesame seeds and has a rich, nutty flavor. It is commonly used as a seasoning in dipping sauces.

Canola This neutral-flavored oil is noted for its monounsaturated fats and is recommended for general cooking.

Chile An infusion of fresh or dried hot red chiles in vegetable oil or sesame oil, this spicy Asian condiment should be used sparingly at first until you become familiar with its heat. Look for it in well-stocked supermarkets and Asian groceries.

Olive This essential ingredient throughout the Mediterranean contributes a delicate, fruity flavor to dishes. Deeply flavorful extra-virgin olive oil is produced from the

first pressing of the olives without the use of heat or chemicals. It has a clear green or brownish hue and a fruity, slightly peppery flavor that is used to best advantage when tossing and dressing pasta that will not be cooked further. Olive oils extracted using heat or chemicals, then filtered and blended to eliminate much of the olives' character, may be used for general cooking purposes. In the past, such oil was labeled "pure olive oil." Today, it is simply labeled "olive oil."

Peanut Pressed from peanuts, this oil has a hint of rich, nutty flavor. It is often used for stir-frying.

Truffle Both black and white truffles, aromatic underground fungi, are rare, highly prized, and expensive. Truffle-infused olive oil captures their evocative fragrance, with the white truffle oil the more strongly scented of the two. To protect the fragile essence of truffle oil, drizzle it on foods just before serving.

OLIVES
Olives are among the oldest and most important of the world's crops, especially throughout the Mediterranean, where they are prized for their oil or are cured.

Gaeta Brownish black and with a nutty flavor, this Italian olive is salt cured, soft, and smooth.

Kalamata The most popular Greek variety, this almond-shaped olive is purplish black, rich, and meaty. It is brine cured and then packed in oil or vinegar.

ONIONS
This humble bulb vegetable, in the same family as leeks and garlic, is one of the most common ingredients in the kitchen.

Green Also known as scallions or spring onions, green onions are the immature shoots of the bulb onion, with a narrow white base that has not yet begun to swell and long, flat green leaves. They are mild in flavor and are common ingredients in Asian recipes, often as a garnish.

Yellow The yellow globe onion is the familiar, all-purpose onion sold in supermarkets. It can be globular, flattened, or slightly elongated and has parchmentlike golden brown skin. Yellow onions are usually too harsh for serving raw, but they become rich and sweet when cooked.

PANCETTA This flavorful Italian bacon, which derives its name from *pancia*, the Italian word for "belly," has a moist, silky texture. It is made by rubbing a slab of pork belly with a simple mixture of spices, and then rolling the slab into a tight cylinder and curing it for at least 2 months.

PASTA See page 18 for information on fresh and dried pasta varieties.

PINE NUTS These small nuts have an elongated, slightly tapered shape and a delicate, resinous flavor. Purchase pine nuts from markets with a good turnover, as they have a short shelf life due to their naturally high concentration of oil. Store the nuts in an airtight container in a cool place away from light for shorter periods, or in the refrigerator or freezer for longer periods.

PROSCIUTTO This Italian ham is a seasoned, salt-cured, air-dried rear leg of pork. Prosciutto is not smoked or cooked, and it is treated with a minimum of salt, but it is cured enough to be eaten without cooking. The result is a meat with a distinctive fragrance and a subtle flavor. Aged from 10 months to 2 years, prosciutto from Parma in the Italian region of Emilia-Romagna is considered the best.

RED PEPPER FLAKES These flakes and seeds result from crushing dried red chiles. Red pepper flakes are a popular seasoning in Italy, especially in the south. Just a pinch or two will add a bit of heat to a pasta sauce.

SALT, KOSHER A favorite of many cooks, kosher salt has large flakes that are easy to grasp between fingertips. This coarse salt, made by compressing granular salt, is available free of additives. Kosher salt has a superior flavor to table salt. It is also not as salty as table salt and thus can be used more liberally. Sea salt may be substituted.

SERRANO CHILE This fresh hot chile is similar to the more familiar jalapeño variety in heat intensity and appearance, although it is smaller and more slender. It can be green or red. After working with hot chiles such as serrano, be careful not to touch any sensitive areas, especially your eyes or mouth, and be sure to wash your hands, the cutting board, and knife well with plenty of hot, soapy water. Capsaicin, the compound that gives chiles their heat, can linger on these surfaces. If you want to lessen the heat of a chile in your dish, remove the white membranes and seeds from its interior. This is where most of the capsaicin is concentrated.

SHALLOTS These small members of the onion family look like large cloves of garlic covered with papery bronze or reddish skin. Shallots have white flesh streaked with purple, a crisp texture, and a flavor more subtle than that of onions. They are often used for flavoring recipes that would be overpowered by the stronger taste of onion.

SHRIMP Shrimp are often sold peeled and deveined. However, it's best to purchase shrimp still in their shells if possible. Most shrimp have been previously frozen, and the shells help preserve their texture and flavor. To peel and devein shrimp at home, first cut off the head if it is still attached. Carefully pull off the legs on the inside of the curve of the shrimp. Starting at the head, carefully pull away the shell from the meat; pull off the tail too, unless otherwise directed. Using a paring knife, make a shallow cut down the back of each shrimp. With the tip of the knife, lift out and gently scrape away the dark veinlike intestinal tract.

SOY SAUCE This pungent, salty sauce, made from fermented soybeans, wheat, and water, comes in various types, from light and mild to dark and intense. Japanese soy sauce tends to be milder tasting, slightly sweeter, and less salty than other varieties.

SQUASH, BUTTERNUT This large winter squash has beige skin and orange-yellow flesh. It is identifiable by the round bulb at one end. When baked, butternut squash has flavorful, dense flesh that can be used to fill ravioli or tortellini.

TOMATO PASTE This dense purée is made from slow-cooked tomatoes that have been strained and cooked down to a deep red concentrate. Tomato paste has a low acid and high sugar content and is sold in tubes, tins, and jars.

TOMATOES, PLUM These egg-shaped tomatoes, also known as Roma tomatoes, have meaty, flavorful flesh prized particularly for making sauce. When buying fresh plum tomatoes, look for fragrant, evenly colored specimens. For canned plum tomatoes or those packaged in aseptic boxes, look for brands low in sodium and other additives. The imported Italian varieties, usually labeled "Italian peeled tomatoes," often offer the best quality. Canned tomatoes should be tender, red from end to end, and packed in natural juices that are neither watery nor too thick.

VINEGAR, RICE Produced from fermented rice and widely used in Asian cuisines, rice vinegar adds a slight acidity to dipping sauces. It is available plain or sweetened; the latter is labeled "seasoned rice vinegar."

WASABI Similar to horseradish, this pungent Japanese root is commonly sold as a green powder that can be reconstituted with water. Wasabi is often served as a condiment alongside Japanese noodles and sushi.

WHITE PEPPER Made from black peppercorns that have had their skins removed before the berries are dried, white pepper is often less aromatic and milder in flavor than black pepper. It is favored in the preparation of light-colored sauces.

ZEST The zest is the outer colored portion of citrus rind, which is rich in flavorful oils. You can easily remove zest with a rasp grater or the finest rasps on a box grater-shredder, but be careful to remove just the colored portion and not the bitter white pith underneath. When choosing citrus for zesting, look for organic fruit, since pesticides concentrate in the thin skins of fruits.

Index

_f_P

FREE PRESS

A Division of Simon & Schuster, Inc.
1230 Avenue of the Americas
New York, NY 10020

WILLIAMS-SONOMA

Founder & Vice-Chairman Chuck Williams

WELDON OWEN INC.

Chief Executive Officer John Owen
President and Chief Operating Officer Terry Newell
Chief Financial Officer Christine E. Munson
Vice President International Sales Stuart Laurence
Creative Director Gaye Allen
Publisher Hannah Rahill
Senior Editor Jennifer Newens
Editor Heather Belt
Editorial Assistant Juli Vendzules
Art Director Kyrie Forbes
Designers Marisa Kwek and Adrienne Aquino
Production Director Chris Hemesath
Color Manager Teri Bell
Production and Reprint Coordinator Todd Rechner
Food Stylist Alison Attenborough
Prop Stylist Marina Malchin
Assistant Food Stylist Colin Flynn
Assistant Food Stylist and Hand Model Brittany Williams
Photographer's Assistant Mario Jimenez

PHOTO CREDITS

Jeff Kauck, all photography, except the following:
Bill Bettencourt: Pages 33 (bottom right),
40 (cleaning mushrooms sequence), 45, and 132.
Mark Thomas: Pages 42, 43, 44, and 133 (top left and top right).

THE MASTERING SERIES

Conceived and produced by Weldon Owen Inc.
814 Montgomery Street, San Francisco, CA 94133
Telephone: 415 291 0100 Fax: 415 291 8841

In collaboration with Williams-Sonoma, Inc.
3250 Van Ness Avenue, San Francisco, CA 94109

A WELDON OWEN PRODUCTION
Copyright © 2005 by Weldon Owen Inc. and Williams-Sonoma Inc.

All rights reserved, including the right of reproduction in whole or in part
in any form.

FREE PRESS and colophon are registered trademarks of Simon & Schuster, Inc.

For information regarding special discounts for bulk purchases,
please contact Simon & Schuster Special Sales at 1 800 456 6798 or
business@simonandschuster.com

Set in ITC Berkeley and FF The Sans.

Color separations by Embassy Graphics.
Printed and bound in China by SNP Leefung Printers Limited.

First printed in 2005.

10 9 8 7 6 5 4 3 2 1

Library of Congress Cataloging-in-Publication data is available.

ISBN–13: 978-0-7432-6734-2
ISBN–10: 0-7432-6734-6

ACKNOWLEDGMENTS

Weldon Owen wishes to thank the following people for their
generous support in producing this book: Carrie Bradley,
David Cannon, Ken DellaPenta, Leslie Evans, Emily Jahn, Karen Kemp,
Shana Lopes, M. Bridget Maley, Cynthia Scheer, Jes Schneider,
Laura Shear, Sharon Silva, Bob Simmons, Coleen Simmons, and
David Vardy of O Chamé restaurant in Berkeley, CA.

A NOTE ON WEIGHTS AND MEASURES

All recipes include customary U.S. and metric measurements. Metric conversions are based on
a standard developed for these books and have been rounded off. Actual weights may vary.